STEAM LOCOMOTIVES 1955

60,000 – 69,999

EASTERN,
NORTH EASTERN
AND SCOTLAND

ERIC SAWFORD

ALAN SUTTON PUBLISHING LIMITED

First published in the United Kingdom in 1994 by
Alan Sutton Publishing Ltd · Phoenix Mill · Far Thrupp · Stroud
Gloucestershire

First published in the United States of America in 1994 by
Alan Sutton Publishing Inc. · 83 Washington Street · Dover · NH 03820

British Library Cataloguing in Publication Data

Sawford, E. H.
  Steam Locomotives, 1955: 60,000–69,999
  – Eastern, North Eastern and Scotland
  I. Title
  625.2610941

ISBN 0–7509–0408–9

Library of Congress Cataloging in Publication Data applied for

Typeset in 10/12 pt Palatino.
Typesetting and origination by
Alan Sutton Publishing Limited.
Printed in Great Britain by
Butler & Tanner, Frome, Somerset.

Contents

Cambridge depot E4s were used on many duties, including the Colchester trains and several local branch lines. In the early fifties they were frequently to be seen on station pilot duties, as was the case with no. 62783. This example, built at Stratford in 1894, was withdrawn in December 1954
13.7.54

Introduction

Although not readily apparent at the time, 1955 was an important landmark in the long history of the steam locomotive on British Railways. Many pre-grouping locomotives – some dating back to the 1880s – were still in daily use, while others continued to receive a general works overhaul, almost certainly their last.

All this was to change in a very short period of time. British Railways Standard designs were being built, which were mainly passenger and freight engines, and replaced many of the pre-grouping examples. Even more important were the huge numbers of diesel locomotives that were being constructed. Many of these were designed for shunting work, but before long they had replaced a lot of steam locomotives – often these were to be seen lying idle or in storage, many destined to do little or no work again. Numerous classes familiar for years became increasingly extinct.

During the fifties many 4–4–0 designs were still in service: these were often used on cross-country routes or branch line work, as indeed were various other smaller wheel arrangements. The introduction of diesel multiple units was to quickly change all this, as they rapidly took over services. Many line closures made even more locomotives redundant, especially at the end of the decade.

At the start of the sixties the remaining steam locomotive stock presented a very different picture. Gone forever were many favourite classes; others were reduced to a handful of examples which saw little use, as apart from enthusiasts' specials. Most of the locomotives that remained were of standard or modern designs from the 'Big Four' days. There were of course exceptions where older engines were still in use, often on special duties.

During 1955 one could still find many examples of wheel arrangements in service which would disappear completely in the next three or four years. One of these was the 2–4–0, the E4 class introduced by J. Holden for the Great Eastern Railway in 1891. This class was still to be found in use, although its duties were being taken over by more modern motive power. The last survivor of the other 2–4–0 class, the three Midland and South Western Joint engines, had been withdrawn the previous year. Another Great Eastern class destined to disappear quickly was the Y4 short wheelbase 0–4–0Ts, all of which were to be found at Stratford. These were introduced in 1913, but by 1957 all had gone. At Aberdeen four 0–4–2Ts of two classes, Z4 and Z5, were still in use at Aberdeen Docks. These engines were all built by Manning Wardle of Leeds in 1915 for the Great North of Scotland Railway. Even as early as 1955 there were normally only two working on a daily basis, depending on the traffic flow in the docks. At the end of the same year the massive LNER class U1 'Beyer-Garratt' locomotive no. 69999 was also withdrawn.

These were just a few examples of the fascinating locomotives to be seen at that time, though there were of course many more. On occasions you could visit a depot or maybe happen to be at the lineside with a camera and be lucky enough to catch a veteran locomotive. Needless to say the opportunity of recording on film was always taken whenever possible.

Steam locomotives were always an attraction for me, ever since my earliest years. In the forties cameras and film were very expensive and difficult to come by, and in any case railway photography was not permissible during the war years. In 1950 I reached an important decision, in that unlike most of my contemporaries, who were interested in collecting numbers, I would set out to record on film as many of the locomotive types and variations as I could. Not just the Eastern Region ones I hasten to add, but from all regions. While I perhaps did not fully realize it at the time, it was a very formidable task.

Railway photography was very different in the fifties to what it is today. Individual permits could be obtained for visits to Western, Southern, London Midland and Scottish Region depots. However, the Eastern and North Eastern Regions would only permit visits by organized parties. Unless you were lucky enough to find a cooperative running foreman, visits to these depots presented problems. At many the layout of the shed itself was a drawback! For example at New England access was over a footbridge in full view of the shed master's office. You had no chance in the fifties if you were on your own, except perhaps if you were very lucky on a Sunday.

In those distant days you could apply for a lineside photographic permit. The quality of the work you submitted with your application would be considered and if you were lucky, subject to an indemnity being signed, a permit for specific sections of line, but not covering access to depots, would be issued, to be reviewed on an annual basis.

Over the years I travelled many miles with my camera, which in those early days was an Agfa Isollete, producing 2¼ in negatives. My travels took me to many places, including Inverness, Aberdeen, Holyhead, Penzance, Brighton and Newcastle. Usually at each town I would add something to my collection. On numerous occasions I have found a particular locomotive, which I especially wished to photograph, at the back of a dark shed, maybe not having been steamed for some considerable time. It was not unknown at this time for a cooperative member of staff to have the engine towed out to enable it to be photographed.

My collection grew in size, but I did not think that the pictures I had taken would be of very much interest to others. How wrong I was – as steam locomotives were withdrawn, enthusiasts would travel long distances to see what in the fifties were commonplace. Often at that time when visiting a depot a class 5 or 4F 0–6–0 would be outside in immaculate condition, while preference would be given to an ageing locomotive often in a very shabby condition. Remember film was not cheap in the fifties so a difficult choice would have to be made. On many occasions in recent years I have seen something in the background of my pictures – and wondered why I did not take a photograph of that as well!

My intention in writing this book is to convey to readers using my own pictures, the fascinating array of locomotive types which were still in service at the end of December 1955. Not every example can be covered. In some classes almost every locomotive was different in one way or another: chimney types, steam brake only, vacuum ejector fitted, tender types and so on. However, all the main locomotives that remained in service are covered as far as possible within the space allowed. The book is not intended to be a reference book of exactly what locomotives were still in service, but it does give many interesting facts on the various locomotive classes – their designer, introduction and principal dimensions – and other interesting comments.

I now turn to the preservation scene. Unlike the Southern, Western and London Midland, the regions covered in this book did not have a 'Barry Yard'. Instead there were private scrapyards where, unlike the well-known South Wales yard, locomotives were cut up either as soon as received or very shortly afterwards. Many of the engines that were condemned before the mass withdrawals of the sixties were sent to one of the locomotive works for scrapping where they did not last long.

Fortunately, while we do not have in preservation a large number of the locomotive types which appear in this book, we do have a representative selection. From the North British designs, there is a 'Glen' 4–4–0, J36 0–6–0 and Y9 0–4–0ST. The North Eastern is represented by examples of the powerful Q6 and Q7 0–8–0s together with a J21 and J27 0–6–0, not forgetting the sturdy J72 0–6–0T no. 69023, built in 1951 to a design originally introduced in 1898, and two Y class 0–4–0Ts. The Great Eastern has the E4 2–4–0 locomotives, often referred to as 'Intermediates', and a J69 0–6–0T and J17 0–6–0, all part of the National Collection at York Railway Museum. Sole survivors of the once numerous N7 0–6–2T, J15 0–6–0 and B12 4–6–0 are to be seen at preserved lines and there is the exciting prospect of the B12 being in action in the near future after a great many years. The Great Northern Railway has not fared so well: of the types still working in 1955 only a J52 ST and N2 0–6–2T survive. Luckily the two famous 'Atlantics' are preserved: no. 990 *Henry Oakley* and C1 class no. 251. The graceful Great North of Scotland D40 4–4–0 is to be seen at the Glasgow Museum of Transport while the Great Central has a D11 ('Director') 4–4–0 and one of the powerful 2–8–0 O4 class.

From the LNER days six of H.N. Gresley's magnificent A4s survive, two of which are in preservation on the other side of the North Atlantic. Two other 'Pacifics' are with us today, the legendary *Flying Scotsman* and *Blue Peter*, both superbly restored and from time to time seen at the head of enthusiasts' specials. Only one of the 'War Winners', as they were often referred to, from Gresley's V2 class 2–6–2 is with us today: luckily it is *Green Arrow* itself which has survived. Two B1s, a K1 2–6–0 and K4 *The Great Marquess*, D49 4–4–0 *Morayshire* and a Y1 Sentinel complete the picture. In addition there are the various preserved locomotives, mostly part of the National Collection, which were withdrawn many years ago. To add variety a few pictures of preserved locomotives have been included.

There are many very worthy designs no longer with us, which appear in this book: 'Clauds', K3 2–6–0s, 'Sandringhams', no doubt the list could be endless. We are, however, fortunate to have those examples mentioned preserved as part of the National Collection. We are also indebted to individuals and preservation societies who have managed to save examples before it was too late.

Eric Sawford
May 1994

Gresley 'Pacific' Nameplates

Many of the A4s were named after birds. No. 60024 *Kingfisher* was one of the last members of the class in service, being withdrawn in September 1966 and ending its days in a County Durham scrapyard

The nameplate of A3 class no. 60037 *Hyperion*, named after the winner of the 1933 Derby and St Leger

A3 class no. 60071 *Tranquil*, named after the winner of two famous races, the St Leger and 1,000 Guineas in 1923. Note the LNER plate

A4 class 4–6–2 8P 'Pacific'

Designer: H.N. Gresley. Introduced in 1935. Streamlined design.
Total built: 35, 1935–8 at Doncaster works. All named. One member of the class was destroyed in an air raid at York in 1942.

Principal dimensions

Weight:	Locomotive	102 tons 19 cwt
	Tender	60 tons 7 cwt
		64 tons 19 cwt (corridor type)
Boiler pressure:		250 lb/sq in
Driving wheels:		6 ft 8 in
Tractive effort:		35,455 lb
Cylinders:		(3) 18½ in x 26 in

Walschaerts valve gear and derived motion – piston valves.

60001	*Sir Ronald Matthews*		60018	*Sparrow Hawk*
60002	*Sir Murrough Wilson*		60019	*Bittern*
60003	*Andrew K. McCosh*		60020	*Guillemot*
60004	*William Whitelaw*		60021	*Wild Swan*
60005	*Sir Charles Newton*		60022	*Mallard*
60006	*Sir Ralph Wedgwood*		60023	*Golden Eagle*
60007	*Sir Nigel Gresley*		60024	*Kingfisher*
60008	*Dwight D. Eisenhower*		60025	*Falcon*
60009	*Union of South Africa*		60026	*Miles Beevor*
60010	*Dominion of Canada*		60027	*Merlin*
60011	*Empire of India*		60028	*Walter K. Whigham*
60012	*Commonwealth of Australia*		60029	*Woodcock*
60013	*Dominion of New Zealand*		60030	*Golden Fleece*
60014	*Silver Link*		60031	*Golden Plover*
60015	*Quicksilver*		60032	*Gannet*
60016	*Silver King*		60033	*Seagull*
60017	*Silver Fox*		60034	*Lord Faringdon*

These fine locomotives were undoubtedly Sir Nigel Gresley's finest design. His long career as locomotive superintendent and chief mechanical engineer commenced in 1911 with the Great Northern Railway and lasted until 1941. The most famous of all the class is no. 60022 *Mallard* which achieved the world speed record for steam in July 1938.

The pre-war exploits of these locomotives on such crack express trains as the 'Silver Jubilee' have been well documented. After the war considerable time was needed to catch up with maintenance of both locomotives and track. In 1948 through, non-stop workings were restored between London and Edinburgh. These duties were in the very capable hands of the A4s with 'Top Link' locomotives from King's Cross and Haymarket depots performing magnificently right through until they were replaced by diesel power in 1961. The final duties for some of the last A4s in use were on the Glasgow–Aberdeen services.

Withdrawals commenced in 1962; the last to go were no. 60019 *Bittern* and no. 60024 *Kingfisher* in September 1966. Fortunately six have been preserved, two of which are overseas: 60008 *Dwight D. Eisenhower* (United States of America) and 60010 *Dominion of Canada* (Canada). The remaining four are: 60007 *Sir Nigel Gresley*, 60009 *Union of South Africa* (both of which are in working order and are regularly to be seen on enthusiasts' specials), 60019 *Bittern* and 60022 *Mallard*, the world steam record holder itself which is to be seen on display at the National Railway Museum, York.

While the A4s were in charge of many of the principal express workings on the East Coast main line, during the fifties and early sixties they could also, on occasions, be seen on everyday duties. Here no. 60032 *Gannet* approaches Huntingdon with a Sunday King's Cross–Peterborough local
11.7.54

During the final years of steam many enthusiasts' specials were organized. One such was by the
A4 Preservation Society when no. 60024 *Kingfisher* was bought down from Aberdeen to work a
Waterloo–Weymouth special, this fine engine providing a magnificent run on the return from
Salisbury to Waterloo. Here the locomotive is seen taking water on the outward journey

26.3.66

No. 60034 *Lord Faringdon*, seen here leaving Huntingdon, was in immaculate condition. This was
for many years one of the King's Cross depot 'Top Link' engines. Its final years were spent at
Aberdeen from where it was withdrawn in August 1966

21.6.57

This picture of the most famous of all the A4s, no. 60022 *Mallard*, was taken in the yard at York Museum prior to many of the exhibits moving to Swindon while the museum was rebuilt. The A4 together with 'Atlantic' no. 251 and 'Crab' no. 2700 were ready to be towed by no. 47375 *Tinsley Traction Depot*. The A4 and other locomotives returned when the museum building was ready to accept exhibits

23.3.91

This rather strange scene of A4 no. 60032 *Gannet* was taken at Doncaster shed. The locomotive was receiving attention to the rear pair of driving wheels at the time and was temporarily standing in the shed yard

10.11.57

Diverted to the 'down slow' due to Sunday engineering work no. 60006 *Sir Ralph Wedgwood* heads a King's Cross–Harrogate train slowly through Huntingdon station. Note the large dent in the casing between the buffers. No. 60006 ended its days at Aberdeen being withdrawn in September 1965

2.10.55

One of the two working examples of the A4 class is no. 4498 *Sir Nigel Gresley* (no. 60007). This photograph of the superbly restored locomotive was taken at Peterborough in the year following its withdrawal from BR service

1.10.67

A3 class 4–6–2 7P 'Pacific'

Introduced in 1927. This design was a development of the original Gresley 'Pacific' which made its appearance in 1922 for the Great Northern Railway.
Designer: H.N. Gresley.
Total built: 78. All named.

Principal dimensions

Weight:	Locomotive	96 tons 5 cwt
	tender	57 tons 18 cwt
	GN type	56 tons 6 cwt
Boiler pressure:		220 lb/sq in
Driving wheels:		6 ft 8 in
Tractive effort:		32,910 lb
Cylinders:		(3) 19 in x 26 in

Walschaerts valve gear and derived motion – 8 in piston valves.

60035	Windsor Lad	60066	Merry Hampton
60036	Colombo	60067	Ladas
60037	Hyperion	60068	Sir Visto
60038	Firdaussi	60069	Sceptre
60039	Sandwich	60070	Gladiateur
60040	Cameronian	60071	Tranquil
60041	Salmon Trout	60072	Sunstar
60042	Singapore	60073	St Gatien
60043	Brown Jack	60074	Harvester
60044	Melton	60075	St Frusquin
60045	Lemberg	60076	Galopin
60046	Diamond Jubilee	60077	The White Knight
60047	Donovan	60078	Night Hawk
60048	Doncaster	60079	Bayardo
60049	Galtee More	60080	Dick Turpin
60050	Persimmon	60081	Shotover
60051	Blink Bonny	60082	Neil Gow
60052	Prince Palatine	60083	Sir Hugo
60053	Sansovino	60084	Trigo
60054	Prince of Wales	60085	Manna
60055	Woolwinder	60086	Gainsborough
60056	Centenary	60087	Blenheim
60057	Ormonde	60088	Book Law
60058	Blair Athol	60089	Felstead
60059	Tracery	60090	Grand Parade
60060	The Tetrarch	60091	Captain Cuttle
60061	Pretty Polly	60092	Fairway
60062	Minoru	60093	Coronach
60063	Isinglass	60094	Colorado
60064	Tagalie	60095	Flamingo
60065	Knight of Thistle	60096	Papyrus

60097	*Humorist*	60105	*Victor Wild*
60098	*Spion Kop*	60106	*Flying Fox*
60099	*Call Boy*	60107	*Royal Lancer*
60100	*Spearmint*	60108	*Gay Crusader*
60101	*Cicero*	60109	*Hermit*
60102	*Sir Frederick Banbury*	60110	*Robert the Devil*
60103	*Flying Scotsman*	60111	*Enterprise*
60104	*Solario*	60112	*St Simon*

The majority were built by Doncaster works, with the exception of twenty built at the Hyde Park works of the North British Locomotive Co. Only those built from 1928 to 1935 were constructed as A3 class. No. 60097 *Humorist* received a double chimney in 1937; it was not until 1958 that the remainder started to receive them, and all were eventually fitted out. In 1960 'Trough Type' smoke deflectors were fitted to two locomotives; all but twenty-three of the class were eventually to receive them.

During the fifties A3s were responsible for many express trains on the East Coast main line and in Scotland. Visits to Doncaster works could usually be relied upon to produce at least one rare example from north of the border. In the process of receiving a general overhaul, some completed and freshly painted at the motive power depot on running in turns, or ready to return north to its home depot. Occasionally before they were sent home one or two worked in the south. This was usually the only time that those from Carlisle Canal depot were seen in the capital.

While 'Pacifics' often worked the fast freight and parcels traffic, these were frequently booked return workings. By the end of the fifties A3s were becoming more common on these duties together with local passenger trains.

The first A3 to be withdrawn was no. 60104 *Solario* in December 1959. In the early sixties diesel locomotives were becoming available in ever increasing numbers, especially on the East Coast main line, taking over many of the duties worked by the A3s. As withdrawals started to gather pace, some locomotives were to find themselves in new areas. Among these were those working passenger trains on the Midland main line north of Leeds; others were transferred north of the border.

The one preserved A3, no. 60103 *Flying Scotsman* was withdrawn from service in working order in January 1963. The last three A3s were all allocated to St Margaret's shed (Edinburgh): these were *Salmon Trout*, *Prince Palatine* and *Spearmint*, two of which were withdrawn in 1965. The last survivor, no. 60052 *Prince Palatine* was withdrawn in January 1966 and was cut up eight months later.

Fortunately we have one survivor of this famous class, which has become possibly the most widely known locomotive in preservation. Now restored to its British Railways livery complete with double chimney and smoke deflectors, the *Flying Scotsman* is how many people will remember the A3s.

No. 60050 *Persimmon* awaits its next duty at Sheffield Darnall shed. This locomotive was withdrawn in June 1963. In its later days it was often to be seen on local passenger workings between King's Cross and Peterborough

24.6.56

Darlington shed usually had an A3 in steam on standby to take over an express from a failed engine. No. 60071 *Tranquil*, one of the batch built by the North British Locomotive Co. was carrying out this duty when photographed

7.7.56

A3 no. 60106 *Flying Fox* blasts through Huntingdon with a northbound express, as was typical of the A3s in the fifties. This particular locomotive later received a double chimney and smoke deflectors. In its last years *Flying Fox* was used on several occasions on enthusiasts' specials

c. 1952

Time was running out for no. 60102 *Sir Frederick Banbury*, seen here passing Huntingdon with a 'Down Express': within two months this locomotive was withdrawn. This particular A3 was one which never received the German-type smoke deflectors

9.61

A3 no. 60036 *Colombo*, bright as a new pin at Doncaster shed on a grey November day. This locomotive was one of the batch built from new as A3s, in this case being completed in July 1934 and remaining in service until November 1964

10.11.57

No. 60112 *St Simon* presented a rather sorry sight at York. The engine was allocated to New England at this time. The remaining A3s spent the last days on occasional passenger, parcels and goods trains. *St Simon* had received a coat of paint at the bottom of the smokebox door to cover the signs of hard running. At the end of 1964 this A3 was withdrawn

2.5.64

Withdrawn and awaiting its last journey no. 60065 *Knight of Thistle* stands in the almost deserted New England shed yards. The following month it was towed to Kings of Norwich for scrapping. It is a great pity that at least one other member of this famous class was not preserved

30.8.64

At Heaton shed visitors could find A3s and other 'Pacifics' from Scotland and the English depots. No. 60099 *Call Boy* was an Edinburgh engine. Note the banjo-shaped dome and straight-sided tender

8.7.56

A1/1 class 4–6–2 8P

The prototype of the A1 class was no. 60113 *Great Northern*, rebuilt in 1945 by E Thompson. In 1947 this locomotive became class A1/1. During the late fifties it was allocated to Doncaster depot, remaining in service until November 1962 and being cut up at Doncaster works in February 1963. The main dimensions below were the same for no. 60113 except for the locomotive weight which was 101 tons.

60113   *Great Northern*

A1 class

These were the A.H. Peppercorn development of the A1/1 class above. Five were fitted with roller bearings nos. 60153–7. BR nos. 60114–60162.
Designer: A.H. Peppercorn.
Total built: 49 at Doncaster and Darlington works 1948–9. All named.

Principal dimensions

Weight:	Locomotive	104 tons 2 cwt
	Tender	60 tons 7 cwt
Boiler pressure:		250 lb/sq in
Driving wheels:		6 ft 8 in
Tractive effort:		37,400 lb
Cylinders:		(3) 19 in x 26 in

Walschaerts motion – piston valves.

60114	*W.P. Allen*		60133	*Pommern*
60115	*Meg Merrilies*		60134	*Foxhunter*
60116	*Hal o' the Wynd*		60135	*Madge Wildfire*
60117	*Bois Roussel*		60136	*Alcazar*
60118	*Archibald Sturrock*		60137	*Redgauntlet*
60119	*Patrick Stirling*		60138	*Boswell*
60120	*Kittiwake*		60139	*Sea Eagle*
60121	*Silurian*		60140	*Balmoral*
60122	*Curlew*		60141	*Abbotsford*
60123	*H.A. Ivatt*		60142	*Edward Fletcher*
60124	*Kenilworth*		60143	*Sir Walter Scott*
60125	*Scottish Union*		60144	*King's Courier*
60126	*Sir Vincent Raven*		60145	*Saint Mungo*
60127	*Wilson Worsdell*		60146	*Peregrine*
60128	*Bongrace*		60147	*North Eastern*
60129	*Guy Mannering*		60148	*Aboyeur*
60130	*Kestrel*		60149	*Amadis*
60131	*Osprey*		60150	*Willbrook*
60132	*Marmion*		60151	*Midlothian*

60152	Holyrood		60158	Aberdonian
60153	Flamboyant		60159	Bonnie Dundee
60154	Bon Accord		60160	Auld Reekie
60155	Borderer		60161	North British
60156	Great Central		60162	Saint Johnstoun
60157	Great Eastern			

The A1s were to be found in all three regions. Shortly after their introduction the class was fitted with double chimneys and Kylchap cowls. These powerful locomotives were to be seen on many of the principal express trains.

The A1s remained intact until 1962, with the withdrawal of 60123 *H.A. Ivatt* following an accident at Offord near Huntingdon. The final survivors were allocated to the North East, the last being no. 60145 *Saint Mungo*, which was withdrawn in July 1966 and cut up at Drapers Hull in the following September.

Unfortunately no examples of the A1 class survive although hopefully in the future a brand new locomotive will be completed, so that one of these fine 'Pacifics' will be seen in action again.

No. 60123 *H.A. Ivatt* was the first A1 to be withdrawn, this as a result of an accident at Offord, a few miles south of where this picture was taken. No. 60123 was working a King's Cross–Peterborough semi-fast when photographed leaving Huntingdon

11.7.54

Two of the Peppercorn A1s carried the names of pre-grouping railway companies. One of these was no. 60157 *Great Eastern*; the nameplate with crest can be clearly seen in this picture taken at York. This A1 was a Doncaster engine for several years before being withdrawn from there in January 1965

2.5.64

Fresh from general overhaul at Doncaster works, a shining no. 60155 *Borderer* was still undergoing 'running-in' when photographed. This A1 was completed in September 1949 at Doncaster works, remaining in service until October 1965 at York depot. It was one of the five A1s fitted with roller bearings

24.6.56

In 1945 E. Thompson rebuilt a Gresley 'Pacific' as the prototype of the later A1s. A1/1 no. 60113 *Great Northern* was still a Grantham engine when photographed at Doncaster. Later the same year it was transferred to this depot, where it remained until it was withdrawn in December 1962

25.8.57

A2/3 class 4–6–2 7MT

The first locomotive of this design no. 60500 *Edward Thompson* emerged from Doncaster works in May 1946. This was the forerunner of the fifteen-strong class which also included nos. 60511–24. All were completed between 1946 and 1947.
Designer: E. Thompson.
Total built: 15. All named.

Principal dimensions

Weight:	Locomotive	101 tons 10 cwt
	Tender	60 tons 7 cwt
Boiler pressure:		250 lb/sq in
Driving wheels:		6 ft 2 in
Tractive effort:		40,430 lb
Cylinders:		(3) 19 in x 26 in

Walschaerts motion – piston valves.

60500	Edward Thompson	60518	Tehran
60511	Airborne	60519	Honeyway
60512	Steady Aim	60520	Owen Tudor
60513	Dante	60521	Watling Street
60514	Chamossaire	60522	Straight Deal
60515	Sun Stream	60523	Sun Castle
60516	Hycilla	60524	Herringbone
60517	Ocean Swell		

The A2/3s were to be found in the Eastern, North Eastern and Scottish regions during the fifties, appearing on express, passenger, parcels and fast goods trains. The five locomotives in the Eastern Region were all to end their days at New England. Most of the class were withdrawn between 1962 and 1963. The last two to remain in service were no. 60512 *Steady Aim* and no. 60522 *Straight Deal*; both were withdrawn from Polmadie (Glasgow) in June 1965.

No. 60517 *Ocean Swell* was among a line of 'Pacifics' at Haymarket depot. This was a Newcastle-based engine at the time which had received one of the much more attractive lipped chimneys, greatly improving its appearance. In the last months it was transferred to Tweedmouth from where it was withdrawn in October 1962

21.8.55

One of the batch of A2/3s at New England was no. 60520 *Owen Tudor*, seen here passing Huntingdon with a King's Cross express. This engine was withdrawn from New England in June 1963. After six months storage at Doncaster works it ended its days on the nearby scrap road

11.11.51

The A2/3s from New England were frequent visitors to the North Eastern region, where this picture of no. 60514 *Chamossaire* was taken. The engine is seen with the early lipped chimney. This A2/3 remained in service until February 1963 and was cut up at Doncaster in the following June

8.7.56

A2/1 class 4–6–2 6MT

These four locomotives were developments of the A2/2 class, incorporating the same boiler as was fitted to the V2 2–6–2s. They were introduced by E. Thompson in 1944.
Designer: E. Thompson.
Total built: Four at Darlington works. (Three were built in 1944, one in 1945.) All carried names with Scottish connections. These 'Pacifics' were built in place of the final four V2s.

Principal dimensions

Weight:	Locomotive	98 tons
	Tender	52 tons
Boiler pressure:		225 lb/sq in
Driving wheels:		6 ft 2 in
Tractive effort:		36,385 lb
Cylinders:		(3) 19 in x 26 in

Walschaerts gear – piston valves.

| 60507 | *Highland Chieftain* | 60509 | *Waverley* |
| 60508 | *Duke of Rothesay* | 60510 | *Robert the Bruce* |

Three of these engines were based in Scotland. No. 60508 was the exception: allocated to New England depot it was a frequent visitor to London.

Withdrawals were as follows: no. 60507 in December 1960, no. 60508 in February 1961, no. 60509 in August 1960 and no. 60510 in November 1960.

Only four locomotives comprised class A2/1. Of these only one, no. 60508 *Duke of Rothesay*, was south of the border. Here the locomotive pulls away from Sandy, heading a King's Cross–Peterborough semi-fast. No. 60508 was the last one to remain in service, being withdrawn in February 1961 from New England depot and ending its days at Doncaster

29.4.56

A2/2 class 4–6–2 7MT

This class consisted of six locomotives all rebuilt from the Gresley P2 2–8–2s. Rebuilding commenced in 1943 with *Thane of Fife*; all six were completed by the end of 1944. They received the nos. 60501–6 when taken over by British Railways.
Designer: When rebuilt, E. Thompson.
Total built: 6.

Principal dimensions

Weight:	Locomotive	101 tons 10 cwt
	Tender	60 tons 7 cwt
Boiler pressure:		225 lb/sq in
Driving wheels:		6 ft 2 in
Tractive effort:		40,320 lb
Cylinders:		(3) 20 in x 26 in

Walschaerts gear – piston valves.

60501	*Cock o' the North*
60502	*Earl Marischal*
60503	*Lord President*
60504	*Mons Meg*
60505	*Thane of Fife*
60506	*Wolf of Badenoch*

The P2s were based at Scottish depots when the decision to rebuild them was made. By the early fifties all the rebuilt locomotives were south of the border, nos. 60501/2/3 at York and nos. 60504/5/6 at New England, where they were to remain for the rest of their service. These engines were frequent visitors to London on both expresses and semi-fasts.

Withdrawals were no. 60501 in February 1960, no. 60502 in July 1961, no. 60503 in November 1959, no. 60504 in January 1961, no. 60505 in November 1959 and no. 60506 in April 1961. All were cut up at Doncaster works.

A2/2 class no. 60506 *Wolf of Badenoch* pulls smartly away from Huntingdon with a King's Cross express. The locomotive is fitted with the earlier plain chimney and smokelifters. In their last years the three New England A2/2s were still seen on express work and frequently on Peterborough–King's Cross semi-fasts

10.1.54

The A2/2s were later fitted with lipped chimneys although still retaining smokelifters. No. 60504 *Mons Meg* was photographed at its home depot, New England. These 'Pacifics' were all withdrawn by July 1961

13.3.55

A2 class 4–6–2 7MT

These powerful locomotives were introduced by A.H. Peppercorn in 1947. A2s were originally fitted with single chimneys; only the last example, no. 60539, was fitted with a double chimney from new, while five others received them in 1949 and all the other class members remained unchanged. These locomotives were numbered 60525–39.
Designer: A.H. Peppercorn.
Total built: 15. All named.

Principal dimensions

Weight:	Locomotive	101 tons
	Tender	60 tons 7 cwt
Boiler pressure:		250 lb/sq in
Driving wheels:		6 ft 2 in
Tractive effort:		40,430 lb
Cylinders:		(3) 19 in x 26 in

Walschaerts motion – piston valves.

21

60525	A.H. Peppercorn	60533	Happy Knight
60526	Sugar Palm	60534	Irish Elegance
60527	Sun Chariot	60535	Hornet's Beauty
60528	Tudor Minstrel	60536	Trimbush
60529	Pearl Diver	60537	Bachelor's Button
60530	Sayajirao	60538	Velocity
60531	Bahram	60539	Bronzino
60532	Blue Peter		

Most of the A2s were to be found at Scottish depots. The exceptions were three based at North Eastern region depots and no. 60533 *Happy Knight* which was in the Eastern region, much of its time spent working from the New England shed. One example still survives, no. 60532 *Blue Peter*, the only one of the four types of A2 class 'Pacifics' to do so.

This A2 received a double chimney in December 1949 just after it was completed at Doncaster works. During the mid-fifties no. 60533 *Happy Knight* and three others in the North Eastern region were to be found allocated south of the border. No. 60533 was withdrawn from New England depot in June 1963. The engine is seen here here leaving Huntingdon with a northbound semi-fast, just two months before it was withdrawn. Steam can be seen leaking from many places

21.4.63

Another of the A2s which never received a double chimney was no. 60537 *Bachelor's Button*, seen here on the turntable at Dundee having worked in from Edinburgh. No. 60537 was withdrawn in October 1962 and cut up at Campbells Airdrie after two years in storage

23.8.55

The first locomotive of the Peppercorn A2 class was named after its designer, the chief mechanical engineer of the LNER from 1946 to 1947. No. 60525 *A.H. Peppercorn* had just received an overhaul at Doncaster when this picture was taken. It was an Aberdeen engine for many years, from where it was withdrawn in May 1963

7.11.54

W1 class 4–6–4 8P

Introduced in 1937, the W1 was rebuilt from H.N. Gresley's experimental high-pressure, four-cylinder compound which was introduced in 1929, with a water-tube boiler as no. 10000.

Designer: H.N. Gresley.
Total built: 1

Principal dimensions

Weight:	Locomotive	107 tons 17 cwt
	Tender	60 tons 7 cwt
Boiler pressure:		250 lb/sq in
Driving wheels:		6 ft 8 in
Tractive effort:		41,435 lb
Cylinders:		(3) 20 in x 26 in

Walschaerts valve gear – piston valves.

This locomotive was never named although various suggestions were put forward over the years. In the British Railways numbering scheme it became 60700.

In the fifties this engine was allocated to Doncaster depot. One of its duties was a morning express to King's Cross returning in the early afternoon, the locomotive regularly working this duty for a considerable time. In September 1955 the engine was just leaving Peterborough when a fractured bogie frame lead to its derailment near Westwood Box. In spite of this no. 60700 was returned to traffic several months later and withdrawn in June 1959.

No. 60700 passing Huntingdon at the head of the 3.50 p.m. King's Cross–Doncaster, its regular duty at this time. Unlike most of the A4s the engine was in rather a shabby condition when this picture was taken

2.5.55

V2 class 2–6–2 6MT

These locomotives were undoubtedly one of H.N. Gresleys finest designs. The first V2 made its appearance from Doncaster works in June 1936, this engine being the well-known sole survivor no. 60800 *Green Arrow*, now part of the National Collection at York Railway Museum.

Designer: H.N. Gresley.

Total built: 184 by Doncaster and Darlington works, 1936–44. Seven carried names. Numbered 60800–60983.

Principal dimensions

Weight:	Locomotive	93 tons 2 cwt
	Tender	52 tons
Boiler pressure:		220 lb/sq in
Driving wheels:		6 ft 2 in
Tractive effort:		33,730 lb
Cylinders:		(3) 18½ in x 26 in

Walschaerts motion – piston valves.

60800	*Green Arrow*
60809	*The Snapper, The East Yorkshire Regiment, The Duke of York's Own*
60835	*The Green Howard, Alexandra, Princess of Wales's Own Yorkshire Regiment*
60847	*St Peter's School, York, A.D. 627*
60860	*Durham School*
60872	*King's Own Yorkshire Light Infantry*
60873	*Coldstreamer*

The V2s proved themselves invaluable engines during the war, often being called upon and handling many Herculean tasks very successfully. Over half the class was constructed during wartime.

The class was distributed widely in all three regions. During the fifties V2s would be frequently seen handling the heaviest expresses as well as another of their main duties, parcel trains.

In their final year eight V2s received double chimneys in an attempt to improve steaming due to the deterioration of coal quality.

Withdrawals commenced in 1962 continuing steadily until 1966, when only a few remained in service. No. 60836 was the last survivor, withdrawn in December 1966.

The very versatile V2s were often called upon to work trains at short notice. In 1953, following problems with the Southern Region Bulleid 'Pacifics', six V2s were loaned to Nine Elms depot where they were employed on express passenger and other traffic for several weeks.

No. 60880 was one of the eight V2s which received double chimneys between 1960 and 1961. The locomotive is seen here at Peterborough acting as a 'standby engine', ready to take over at short notice from an ailing locomotive. The V2 had only another year in service, being withdrawn in September 1963 from Doncaster shed and ending its days two months later at the nearby works

6.9.62

King's Cross depot had a number of the famous Gresley V2 2–6–2s in its allocation, whose regular duties included expresses, semi-fasts and fast goods. On a great many occasions they were booked on principal expresses, at other times deputizing for a failed or unavailable locomotive. No. 60914, in immaculate condition, was heading a King's Cross–Peterborough semi-fast at Huntingdon

18.6.57

Locomotives were stabled on either side of running lines at St Margaret's depot. No. 60886 was a Heaton engine; the class was well represented in St Margaret's allocation, with no less than seventeen examples in the mid-fifties. No. 60886 was completed at Darlington in November 1939 and withdrawn in April 1966 from York depot

21.8.55

B1 class 4–6–0 5MT

Designer: E. Thompson. Introduced 1942.
Total built: 410 over ten-year period 1942–52. Numbered 61000–61409.

Principal dimensions

Weight:	Locomotive	71 tons 3 cwt
	Tender	52 tons
Boiler pressure:		225 lb/sq in
Driving wheels:		6 ft 2 in
Tractive effort:		26,880 lb
Cylinders:		(2) 20 in x 26 in

Walschaerts valve gear – piston valves.

61000	Springbok	61030	Nyala
61001	Eland	61031	Reedbuck
61002	Impala	61032	Stembok
61003	Gazelle	61033	Dibatag
61004	Oryx	61034	Chiru
61005	Bongo	61035	Pronghorn
61006	Blackbuck	61036	Ralph Assheton
61007	Klipspringer	61037	Jairou
61008	Kudu	61038	Blacktail
61009	Hartebeeste	61039	Steinbok
61010	Wildebeeste	61040	Roedeer
61011	Waterbuck	61189	Sir William Gray
61012	Puku	61215	William Henton Carver
61013	Topi	61221	Sir Alexander Erskine-Hill
61014	Oribi	61237	Geoffrey H. Kitson
61015	Duiker	61238	Leslie Runciman
61016	Inyala	61240	Harry Hinchliffe
61017	Bushbuck	61241	Viscount Ridley
61018	Gnu	61242	Alexander Reith Gray
61019	Nilghai	61243	Sir Harold Mitchell
61020	Gemsbok	61244	Strang Steel
61021	Reitbok	61245	Murray of Elibank
61022	Sassaby	61246	Lord Balfour of Burleigh
61023	Hirola	61247	Lord Burghley
61024	Addax	61248	Geoffrey Gibbs
61025	Pallah	61249	FitzHerbert Wright
61026	Ourebi	61250	A. Harold Bibby
61027	Madoqua	61251	Oliver Bury
61028	Umseke	61379	Mayflower
61029	Chamois		

Fifty-nine B1s carried names: the majority (forty) were Antelope names; eighteen were named after directors of LNER; and the exception, *Mayflower*, was named as a symbol of the ties between the two towns of Boston.

The first locomotive of the class (LNER 8301) no. 61000 *Springbok* was completed in December 1942. This was the first of a batch of ten built at Darlington works, 1942–44. The appearance of this brand new design at the height of the Second World War, and so quickly after Edward Thompson had succeeded Sir Nigel Gresley, was a remarkable occurrence.

It was not until 1946 that delivery of this important and versatile class began in earnest, both Darlington and Gorton works building batches, together with the North British Locomotive Co. and Vulcan Foundry. The last of this class to be delivered was a North British Locomotive Co. built engine, no. 61399, completed in April 1952.

B1 class locomotives were allocated to depots over a wide area, including the North of Scotland, the North Eastern and Eastern regions. Withdrawals of the class commenced in November 1961, with one exception, no. 61057, which was to see just four years service, being withdrawn in April 1950 as a result of an accident.

Four coal-weighing tenders were fitted to a number of different B1s at various times.

The B1 class was to be found on many types of duties. On the East Coast main line one example was the King's Cross–Cleethorpes route, worked by an Immingham depot B1. This depot maintained their locomotives in good external and mechanical condition. South of Peterborough the train was on a fast timing, the return evening train running non-stop to Huntingdon. Eventually the B1s were replaced by 'Britannia' class locomotives, displaced from elsewhere on the Eastern region. During the fifties fish trains were a common sight on the East Coast main line, B1s from Immingham having taken over these workings from the depot's K3 class 2–6–0s.

B1s were capable of hauling heavy trains, and as a result were frequently commandeered, often at short notice, to work a train in place of a failed 'Pacific'. Parcels traffic was also usually in the hands of this class, together with the Gresley V2 2–6–2s.

In East Anglia the class was a much-needed replacement to the ageing Great Eastern designs, their introduction improving the services, as did the 'Britannias' in their turn.

Many B1s were used on local passenger work wherever they were allocated. On the southern section of the East Coast main line they were commonplace on the King's Cross–Peterborough local services.

This class of locomotive was very popular in all regions, probably none more so than on the Great Central section. Within a short time they were responsible for most of the express and local services. Duties performed in the North Eastern and Scottish regions followed a very similar pattern, in that they replaced many ageing locomotives on passenger, parcel and freight workings.

By the early sixties B1s were being withdrawn in ever increasing numbers. One example, no. 61395, had just over ten years service! In 1963 a decision was made to transfer a number to departmental stock, receiving a new number in the departmental series. These locomotives were employed on carriage heating and as stationary boilers in the Eastern region. One place where several were to be found was at March, two examples on this work lasting until 1968.

Fortunately, two B1 class locomotives have been preserved (a very different number to their contemporaries on the London Midland region, the 'Black 5s', which have nineteen survivors). These are no. 61264 on the Great Central Railway and no. 61306 on the Nene Valley Railway. Both locomotives were built by the North British Locomotive Co. in 1947 and 1948 respectively. One of these survivors, no. 61264, was transferred to departmental stock in November 1965 as no 29, being condemned in July 1967. It ended up as scrap at Barry, the only ex-LNER type to do so, from where it was purchased and moved to the Great Central Railway in 1976.

No. 61306, now numbered 1306, is named *Mayflower*, although this locomotive was not named during its British Railways service. The name was originally carried by no. 61379 which was withdrawn in August 1962. The present *Mayflower* plates are replicas; the originals are both in the United States. At the time of writing neither locomotive is in service.

No. 61274 of Cambridge depot had just received a general overhaul at Darlington works. This locomotive was built by the North British Locomotive Co., being completed in January 1948 and remaining in service until November 1964. Note the electric lighting fitted

8.7.56

Departmental no. 24 (ex-no. 61375) photographed in March locomotive depot yards. Note the electric lighting still fitted; couplings had been removed, as had the vacuum pipes. This B1, built by the North British Locomotive Co., was completed in February 1951, withdrawn from traffic in November 1963 when it was transferred to departmental stock, and finally condemned in April 1966

30.8.64

Four self-weighing tenders were fitted to various B1s during their service. No. 61140, seen leaving Eastfield shed, Glasgow, under the watchful eye of a running foreman, was in company with tender no. 4219

26.8.55

Typical of many of the B1s still in service in 1964, no. 61138 was standing near the overhead water columns at New England in company with the remaining 9Fs. This B1 was a King's Cross engine for several years. The locomotive was withdrawn in January 1965

30.8.64

This picture reveals a wealth of detail on no. 61032 *Stembok*, one of the class members named after the antelope family. The oval Darlington works plate can be seen above the front buffer beam. *Stembok* was one of the lucky ones, completing nineteen years service

Stockton Motive Power depot, 8.7.56

Another of the March departmental locomotives was no. 23, ex no. 61300, seen here receiving attention in the yard. This B1 was built by the North British Locomotive Co. and completed in March 1948. In November 1963 it was transferred to departmental stock until condemned in 1965

30.8.64

Hitchin B1 no. 61091 pulls smartly away from Huntingdon with a King's Cross–Peterborough local passenger. This B1 was one of the 1946 batch built by the North British Locomotive Co.; it was withdrawn from service in September 1962

c. 1955

B1 class locomotives were able to show a fair turn of speed with the King's Cross–Cleethorpes service south of Peterborough. Here no. 61409, the last in the series, heads north with a Cleethorpes relief, near Huntingdon. This Darlington-built locomotive was completed in June 1950 and withdrawn in September 1963

29.4.54

No. 61181 was busy supplying steam at March depot. The B1 had been re-numbered departmental locomotive no. 18. Note the front coupling had been removed, which was usual with these locomotives, so that they could not be used on trains, although they were capable of running under their own steam to locations and for servicing. No. 61181 still carries its front numberplate. Note the large quantities of ash on the front buffer beam

24.1.65

This photograph reveals the clean lines of the B1 class. No. 61267 was awaiting its next duty at Bradford. Note the lion and wheel emblem on the tender. This B1 was one of the batch completed by the North British Locomotive Co. in 1947

13.5.56

B16 class 4–6–0 6MT

These very popular engines first made their appearance in 1919, designed by V. Raven for the North Eastern Railway. All except one, which was a war casualty, were taken over by British Railways, the number series allocated being 61410–78. The B16s were all built at Darlington works.
Designer: V. Raven.
Total built: 70, between 1919 and 1924.

Principal dimensions

Weight:	Locomotive	
	(B16/1)	77 tons 14 cwt
	Tender	46 tons 12 cwt
Boiler pressure:		180 lb/sq in
Driving wheels:		5 ft 8 in
Tractive effort:		30,030 lb
Cylinders:		(3) 18½ in x 26 in

(B16/1) Stephenson motion – piston valves.

Two other class parts existed:
B16/2 Gresley rebuilds – Walschaerts gear and derived motion.
B16/3 Thompson rebuild – Walschaerts gear.

B16s were widely travelled engines and were frequent visitors to Woodford. On rare occasions they were to be seen south of Peterborough and this class was also widely used for summertime excursion traffic.

Withdrawals commenced in 1958 and continued steadily until the last survivor, no. 61435, was withdrawn in July 1964.

No. 61419 was a typical example of the original B16/1, completed at Darlington in November 1920. The engine was one of the large batch allocated to York where this picture was taken. York B16s were frequent visitors to Woodford and occasionally to the East Coast main line, south of Peterborough
23.9.56

Another B16/1, no. 61411, seen here at Starbeck depot. The engine had received some damage to the front of the running plate. This often happened as the result of rough shunting. No. 61411 was completed in August 1920 and remained in service until September 1961

22.5.55

This engine view of B16/3 no. 61454 shows the Walschaerts valve gear; note also the different running plate. No. 61454 was awaiting its return working at Annesley depot. This locomotive was among the last B16s in service, being withdrawn in June 1964

4.4.54

B12 class 4–6–0 4P

These locomotives first made their appearance on the Great Eastern Railway in 1911 to the design of S.D. Holden. Eighty were constructed at Stratford works and by W. Beardmore & Co. with the final batch in 1928 coming from Beyer, Peacock & Co. Withdrawals had commenced before nationalization and only seventy-two were taken over by British Railways. The number series allocated was 61500–61580.

By the end of 1955 all the B12s that remained in service were B12/3s, rebuilds introduced by H.N. Gresley in 1932, with large round-topped boilers and still retaining original valves.

Designer: S.D. Holden.
Total built: 80.

Principal dimensions

Weight:	Locomotive	69 tons 10 cwt
	Tender	39 tons 6 cwt
Boiler pressure:		180 lb/sq in
Driving wheels:		6 ft 6 in
Tractive effort:		21,970 lb
Cylinders:		(2) 20 in x 28 in

Stephenson motion – piston valves.

In their final years the remaining B12s were mostly seen on local passenger workings, as well as excursion and parcel traffic. At the end of December 1959 no. 61572 was the sole surviving member of the class. The engine was allocated to Norwich depot and, surprisingly, remained in service until September 1961. During this time it appeared on several rail tours. Fortunately this engine is preserved and has been at the North Norfolk Railway for many years. Now, despite numerous problems and set-backs, no. 61572 has been overhauled in Germany. Hopefully, in the not too distant future, it will be in action once again.

In the mid-fifties B12s were allocated to several depots, including Stratford, Norwich, Cambridge, Ipswich and Yarmouth Beach. Also, Grantham and Peterborough Spital Bridge from where their duties took them into London Midland Region territory. They were extremely rare on the East Coast Main Line south of Peterborough. At least one of the Grantham engines is known to have reached King's Cross on an express deputizing for a failed locomotive.

Ready to leave Cambridge depot, B12/3 no. 61535 of Ipswich depot stands awaiting the signal to proceed to its train. This B12 was built at Stratford in 1915, remaining in service until December 1959, and was among the last survivors

3.4.55

Members of the B12 class were allocated to Grantham depot. One of these was no. 61553, seen here at Skegness. This engine was one of the batch of twenty constructed by W. Beardmore & Co. in 1920, being rebuilt as a B12/3 in 1937 and withdrawn in August 1958

19.6.55

B17 class 4–6–0 4P

This class was known as 'Sandringhams', introduced in 1928 by H.N. Gresley to provide badly needed motive power on the Great Eastern section. In all, seventy-three were built between 1928 and 1937. Two private companies, North British Locomotive Co. and R. Stephenson & Co., together with Darlington works constructed engines to this design. All were named. Numbered 61600–61672.

In 1945 E. Thompson commenced rebuilding B17s as two-cylinder engines with 100A type boilers. Ten were rebuilt: these are dealt with under the B2 class, under which they were re-classified.

Designer: H.N. Gresley.
Total built: 73.

Driving wheels:	6 ft 8 in
Tractive effort (B17/1):	22,485 lb
Cylinders:	(3) 17½ in x 26 in

Walschaerts gear and derived motion – piston valves.

B17s in service as at 31 December 1955:

61600	Sandringham	61638	Melton Hall
61601	Holkham	61640	Somerleyton Hall
61602	Walsingham	61641	Gayton Hall
61605	Lincolnshire Regiment	61642	Kilverstone Hall
61606	Audley End	61643	Champion Lodge
61608	Gunton	61645	The Suffolk Regiment
61609	Quidenham	61646	Gilwell Park
61610	Honingham Hall	61647	Helmingham Hall
61611	Raynham Hall	61648	Arsenal
61612	Houghton Hall	61649	Sheffield United
61613	Woodbastwick Hall	61650	Grimsby Town
61618	Wynyard Park	61651	Derby County
61619	Welbeck Abbey	61652	Darlington
61620	Clumber	61653	Huddersfield Town
61621	Hatfield House	61654	Sunderland
61622	Alnwick Castle	61655	Middlesbrough
61623	Lambton Castle	61656	Leeds United
61625	Raby Castle	61657	Doncaster Rovers
61626	Brancepeth Castle	61658	The Essex Regiment
61627	Aske Hall	61659	East Anglian
61629	Naworth Castle	61660	Hull City
61630	Tottenham Hotspur	61661	Sheffield Wednesday
61631	Serlby Hall	61662	Manchester United
61633	Kimbolton Castle	61663	Everton
61634	Hinchingbrooke	61664	Liverpool
61635	Milton	61665	Leicester City
61636	Harlaxton Manor	61666	Nottingham Forest
61637	Thorpe Hall	61667	Bradford

| 61668 | Bradford City | | 61670 | City of London |
| 61669 | Barnsley | | 61672 | West Ham United |

Withdrawals of B17s commenced in 1952. Only engines in service at the end of 1955 appear in the list above.

Two locomotives, nos. 61659 and 61670, were streamlined; this steamlining was removed in 1951. Other B17s were fitted with 100A type boilers and classified B17/6, while a further ten were rebuilt to B2 class.

Many of the B17s were allocated to Cambridge and March in the final years. Their duties included passenger, parcels and fast goods workings. Withdrawals proceeded rapidly in the late fifties, the last survivor being no. 61668 *Bradford City*, withdrawn in August 1960. None survive today.

No. 61627 *Aske Hall* was a March-based engine in 1955. Here it stands in the north end bay at Cambridge with a March train going via St Ives. No. 61627 was a B17/6 with 100A (B1-type boiler); a Darlington-built engine, it remained in service until July 1959

10.10.55

Many of the B17s were named after famous football teams. The name *Liverpool* was carried by no. 61664, built by R. Stephenson & Co. in 1937 and withdrawn in June 1960. Note the football below the name. The team colours also appeared below the name plate

B2 class 4–6–0 4P

These ten locomotives were rebuilds of the B17 class. The B2s, designed by E. Thompson, were two-cylinder engines fitted with 100A (B1) boilers. The first locomotive rebuilt was no. 61671 in August 1945.
Designer: E. Thompson.
Total built: 10.

Principal dimensions

Weight:	Locomotive	73 tons 10 cwt
	Tender	52 tons
Boiler pressure:		225 lb/sq in
Driving wheels:		6 ft 8 in
Tractive effort:		24,865 lb
Cylinders:		(2) 20 in x 26 in

Walschaerts gear and derived motion – piston valves.

61603	*Framlingham*		61617	*Ford Castle*
61607	*Blickling*		61632	*Belvoir Castle*
61614	*Castle Hedingham*		61639	*Norwich City*
61615	*Culford Hall*		61644	*Earlham Hall*
61616	*Fallodon*		61671	*Royal Sovereign*

Cambridge depot had no. 61671 *Royal Sovereign* in its allocation: this locomotive was the 'Royal Engine'. When not on special duties it was often to be seen on the Cambridge–King's Cross workings. Eventually these trains were taken over by B1 class 4–6–0s, the 'Sandringhams' only making occasional appearances. In 1956 all the B2s were at Cambridge where they remained for the rest of their service. All were withdrawn by December 1959.

No. 61617 *Ford Castle* was the reserve 'Royal' engine. This B2 was rebuilt at Darlington works in December 1946. It was the first of the ten B2s to be withdrawn in August 1958. The tender fitted to the locomotive, seen here at Cambridge depot, was from a North Eastern C7 'Atlantic'

23.6.57

Many of the B17s carried names of famous country houses. No. 61603 *Framlingham* was named after a famous property in the county of Norfolk

V4 class 2–6–2 5MT

Designer: H.N. Gresley for the LNER. Introduced in 1941.
Total built: 2.

Principal dimensions

Weight:	Locomotive	70 tons 8 cwt
	Tender	42 tons 15 cwt
Boiler pressure:		250 lb/sq in
Driving wheels:		5 ft 8 in
Tractive effort:		27,420 lb
Cylinders:		(3) 15 in x 26 in

Walschaerts valve gear and derived motion – piston valves.

No. 61700 *Bantam Cock* completed in February 1941
No. 61701 completed in March 1941

Both were built at Doncaster works, originally intended as forerunners of a large class of lightweight 2–6–2s. The Thompson B1 4–6–0s were introduced the following year and no more V4s were built. Only the first locomotive was named, although no. 61701 was often unofficially referred to as *Bantam Hen*. In the mid-fifties both engines were to be found at Aberdeen. In 1957 both were withdrawn, no. 61700 in March and no. 61701 in November, rendering the class extinct.

No. 61701 seen under repair at Aberdeen. This was the last of the pair in service, being withdrawn in November 1957. Although never named this engine was often unofficially referred to as *Bantam Hen*

24.8.55

K2 class 2–6–0 4MT

The K2 class were designed by H.N. Gresley and built between 1912 and 1921. Locomotives were constructed at Doncaster works, the North British Locomotive Co. and Kitson & Co., with the class eventually comprising a total of seventy-five, all of which became BR stock.
Designer: H.N. Gresley.
Total built: 75. Numbered 61720–94.

Principal dimensions

Weight:	Locomotive	64 tons 8 cwt
	Tender	43 tons 2 cwt
Boiler pressure:		180 lb/sq in
Driving wheels:		5 ft 8 in
Tractive effort:		23,400 lb
Cylinders:		(2) 20 in x 26 in

Walschaerts gear – piston valves.

A number of engines were transferred to Scotland and received side-window cabs, working on the West Highland line and elsewhere. Thirteen of these engines received names:

61764	*Loch Arkaig*
61772	*Loch Lochy*
61774	*Loch Garry*
61775	*Loch Treig*
61781	*Loch Morar*
61782	*Loch Eil*
61783	*Loch Sheil*
61787	*Loch Quoich*
61788	*Loch Rannoch*
61789	*Loch Laidon*
61790	*Loch Lomond*
61791	*Loch Laggan*
61794	*Loch Oich*

Withdrawals of the K2s commenced in 1955. The last of the class was no. 61756, withdrawn in June 1962; none survive.

No. 61724 of Immingham depot was photographed at March. Note the cleanliness of this K2: during the fifties Immingham engines were normally to be seen in good external condition. No. 61724 was built at Doncaster in 1913, being withdrawn in January 1958

13.3.55

No. 61794 *Loch Oich* at Eastfield was decidedly the worse for wear. The smokebox door was badly scorched indicating hard work; note also the front running plate which was badly bent, probably due to rough shunting. Nevertheless this K2, the last to be built, in this case by Kitson & Co. in 1921, remained in service until July 1960

26.8.55

K2 class locomotives were often used on passenger trains, both regular services and excursion traffic. No. 61745 of Boston shed was pictured at Skegness on a damp, dismal summer's day. No. 61745 was withdrawn in November 1960

19.6.55

On transfer to Scotland several K2s received side-window cabs. Thirteen were also named. Here No. 61789 *Loch Laidon* is seen at its home shed, Eastfield. K2s were used on the West Highland line, the last remaining in use at Mallaig until 1961

26.8.55

K3 class 2–6–0 6MT

The K3s were designed by H.N. Gresley, a development of his earlier GN design. The first ten members of the class were built at Doncaster between 1920 and 1921. Subsequent batches were built at Darlington and Doncaster works, also by Armstrong Whitworth, North British Locomotive Co. and R. Stephenson & Co. The class was not complete until February 1937, when 193 engines were in service. All members of the class came into BR stock and were allocated nos. 61800–61992.

Designer: H.N. Gresley.
Total built: 193.

Principal dimensions

Weight:	Locomotive	72 tons 12 cwt
	Tender	52 tons
Boiler pressure:		180 lb/sq in
Driving wheels:		5 ft 8 in
Tractive effort:		30,030 lb
Cylinders:		(3) 18½ in x 26 in

Walschaerts gear and derived motion – piston valves.

The K3s were easily recognized by the large boiler with a 6 ft diameter. These were among the best Gresley designs. While principally mixed-traffic engines, they were often used on passenger services. One duty on which they were ideal was parcels, another was fish trains. Immingham depot K3s, usually in immaculate condition, regularly worked fast fish trains over the East Coast main line until eventually the duties were taken over by B1 4–6–0s. One locomotive, no. 61863, was rebuilt in 1945, becoming class K5.

K3s, especially when due for works overhaul, could be rough riding. The K3 class was to be found at Eastern, North Eastern and Scottish depots.

The class remained intact until 1959, when no. 61898 was withdrawn in February. Thereafter withdrawals increased rapidly, the last survivors going in 1962; several of these were used as stationary boilers for a short time afterwards. None have survived to be preserved.

No. 61946 of March depot heads a mixed goods train through St Ives – in the early fifties March had a sizeable allocation of K3s. No. 61946 was built by the North British Locomotive Co. in 1935 and withdrawn in June 1962

1.7.54

Resplendent after a general overhaul at Doncaster works no. 61838 was in the row of engines awaiting testing at Doncaster shed. This K3, built at Doncaster in 1925, remained in service until March 1960

24.6.56

No. 61980 was one of the last batch of K3s built at Darlington works, being completed in this case in December 1936. This picture was taken at its home depot, Annesley. The engine is fitted with a straight-sided tender. No. 61980 was one of the last K3s to be withdrawn, in December 1962

4.4.54

The K3 class was frequently to be found on fast goods traffic. This picture of no. 61824 was taken at Huntingdon on a Sunday morning. The train is just leaving after taking water on its way to London. This K3 was built at Darlington in 1924 and was withdrawn in July 1961

11.7.54

K5 class 2–6–0 6MT

In 1945 E. Thompson rebuilt K3 no. 61863 as a two-cylinder engine with B1-type cylinders. Boiler pressure was increased to 225 lb/sq in and a new boiler was constructed, the rebuilt engine having many new parts. The engine was designated K5 class and was completed at Doncaster in June 1945.
Designer: E. Thompson.
Total built: 1.

Principal dimensions

Weight:	Locomotive	71 tons 5 cwt
	Tender	52 tons
Boiler pressure:		225 lb/sq in
Driving wheels:		5 ft 8 in
Tractive effort:		29,250 lb
Cylinders:		(2) 20 in x 26 in

Walschaerts gear – piston valves.

In the mid-fifties no. 61863 was allocated to Stratford. Despite being to all intents and purposes a new engine it only remained in service for fifteen years, being withdrawn in June 1960.

The original intention was to rebuild ten K3s to K5 class. In the end only one locomotive was rebuilt, no. 61863 in 1945, seen here at Stratford. It only lasted fifteen years in service. Many of the K3s were to remain in traffic until 1962

1.7.54

K4 class 2–6–0 6MT

Designer: H.N. Gresley. Introduced in 1937 for use on the West Highland line.
Total built: 6.

Principal dimensions

Weight:	Locomotive	68 tons 8 cwt
	Tender	44 tons 4 cwt
Boiler pressure:		200 lb/sq in
Driving wheels:		5 ft 2 in
Tractive effort:		36,600 lb
Cylinders:		(3) 18½ in x 26 in

Walschaerts valve gear and derived motion – piston valves.

Six were built at Darlington between 1937 and 1938, all carried names. One locomotive, no. 61997 *MacCailin Mor*, was rebuilt in December 1945 and re-classified class K1/1.

61993	*Loch Long*	61996	*Lord of the Isles*
61994	*The Great Marquess*	61998	*MacLeod of MacLeod*
61995	*Cameron of Lochiel*		

Prior to the arrival of the K4 class most of the passenger traffic on the difficult West Highland line was in the hands of D34 class 4–4–0s, often requiring the heavier trains to be double headed. The powerful K4s, with their higher tractive effort and smaller driving wheels made a remarkable difference on the long, steep gradients and curves which are a feature on this line.

The K4s were eventually to find many of their duties taken over by B1 and class 5 4–6–0s. The last working examples of these locomotives were from Thornton depot. Four were withdrawn in October 1961 and the last survivor, no. 61994 *The Great Marquess*, in December of that year. Fortunately it was purchased on withdrawal, overhauled and repainted in LNER livery at Cowlairs works, which had been responsible for the K4s in BR days. In recent years this engine, now carrying its LNER no. 3442, has worked many enthusiasts' specials and is regularly to be seen in action on the Severn Valley Railway.

No. 61998 *MacLeod of MacLeod* replenishes its water supply at Eastfield depot. This locomotive was the last of the class to be constructed, being completed at the end of 1938, and it carried the name *Lord Dunvegan* for its first three months of service. The small driving wheels, which were such an asset on the West Highland line, can be clearly seen in this picture

26.8.55

K1 class 2–6–0 6MT

Designer: A.H. Peppercorn. Introduced in 1949.
Total built: 70.

Principal dimensions

Weight:	Locomotive	66 tons 17 cwt
	Tender	44 tons 4 cwt
Boiler pressure:		225 lb/sq in
Driving wheels:		5 ft 2 in

51

| *Tractive effort*: | 32,080 lb |
| *Cylinders*: | (2) 20 in x 26 in |

Walschaerts valve gear – piston valves.

Seventy locomotives of the K1 class were built new by the North British Locomotive Co. during 1949 and 1950, receiving BR numbers 62001–70.

In addition a K4 class 2–6–0, no. 61997 *MacCailin Mor*, was rebuilt in 1945 by E. Thompson at Doncaster works, eventually becoming class K1/1, the prototype of the new class K1. This locomotive remained in service until June 1961.

The K1s were a very versatile, powerful design and were found in the Eastern, North Eastern and Scottish regions. During the early fifties March depot had the largest allocation of the class, with no less than thirty K1s. Their duties took them far and wide. The heavy freight workings to London were one duty at which the K1s excelled, co-ordinating with the large number of WD 2–8–0s also allocated to the depot at that time.

The class remained intact until 1962. By 1967 only twenty-four remained in service; all were withdrawn that same year. The last survivor, no. 62005, was condemned in December but fortunately has survived to be preserved, becoming well known for working on BR and the North Yorkshire Moors in recent years, resplendent in LNER green livery and carrying no. 2005.

The sole surviving example of the K1 class, no. 2005 is regularly to be seen in action on the North Yorkshire Moors Railway, seen here at Goathland. This example of the class was the last in service, being withdrawn in December 1967

15.5.91

No. 62020, one of the large number of the class allocated to March depot, heads for home with a mixed goods from St Ives. This locomotive was completed in August 1949 and withdrawn in January 1965

17.7.54

The K1 class was also extensively used in the North East, with six being allocated to 51E Stockton depot. No. 62064 was one of these, photographed at its home shed

8.7.56

D40 class 4–4–0 2P

Designer: W. Pickersgill/T.E. Heywood. Introduced in 1899 for the Great North of Scotland Railway.
Total built: 21.

Principal dimensions

Weight:	Locomotive (saturated engines)	46 tons 7 cwt
	(superheated)	48 tons 13 cwt
	Tender	37 tons 8 cwt
Boiler pressure:		165 lb/sq in
Driving wheels:		6 ft 1 in
Tractive effort:		16,185 lb
Cylinders:		(2) 18 in x 26 in

The D40s were a graceful design. Twenty-one engines were built, the earlier saturated Pickersgill engines from 1899 to 1915 as follows: five by Neilson Reid in 1899, four by Inverurie works between 1909 and 1910 and a further four, also at Inverurie, between 1913 and 1915.

The remaining eight engines were different: these were built to the design of T.E. Heywood. All were built as superheated locomotives, six by the North British Locomotive Co. in 1920 and the final two at Inverurie works in 1921. All of these engines carried names.

Three locomotives had already been withdrawn prior to 1948 when British Railways came into being, the remaining eighteen were allocated nos. 62260–79. The named engines which were in service at the end of 1955 were:

62275   *Sir David Stewart*   62277   *Gordon Highlander*

No. 62275 was withdrawn in December 1955 and the last of the original saturated engines, no. 62264, was withdrawn in March 1957, leaving just one of the superheated designs in service, no. 62277 *Gordon Highlander*, built in 1920 and fortunately now preserved in Glasgow Museum of Transport.

In June 1958 no. 62277 *Gordon Highlander* was withdrawn from normal service. It was to emerge the following month as no. 49 in GNSR green livery. For several years it was used on special trains along with other preserved locomotives from pre-grouping Scottish companies.

Several D40s were still active in the Keith area during the mid-fifties although the writing was on the wall for them. No. 62264 is seen here leaving Keith depot for its next duty. This engine was one of the original batch built by Neilson & Co. in 1899: it lasted in service until March 1957, being the last survivor of the saturated engines

24.8.55

D20 class 4–4–0 2P

Designer: Wilson Worsdell. Introduced in 1899 for the North Eastern Railway.
Total built: 60.

Principal dimensions

Weight:	Locomotive	54 tons 2 cwt (std locos)
	Tender	41 tons 4 cwt (std locos)
Boiler pressure:		175 lb/sq in
Driving wheels:		6 ft 10 in
Tractive effort:		17,025 lb
Cylinders:		(2) 19 in x 26 in

Stephenson valve gear – piston valves.

Sixty of these locomotives were built at Gateshead works from 1899 to 1907. Of these, all but ten were taken into British Railway stock. Nineteen members of the class were withdrawn in 1951, and others steadily throughout the following years, until the last survivors were withdrawn in late 1957. BR numbers allocated to this class was 62340–97.

The D20s were a successful and reliable class designed for express passenger work and would have been an ideal candidate for preservation, alongside the other North Eastern 4–4–0, later to become class D17 at York Museum. By the fifties many of the duties previously worked by these locomotives had been taken over by other classes, although they did have some regular turns right up until the last six were withdrawn. Many of the later examples were principally used on specials and summer excursion traffic.

As with other classes, during their years in service various modifications were made. All were superheated. Four locomotives were rebuilt with long travel valves, becoming class D20/2, all of which were still in service when taken over by British Railways.

During the mid-fifties members of the class could usually be found in Selby depot yard. Among the principal workings of these locomotives were local passenger trains, and holiday traffic to and from the coastal resorts. No. 62345 was built in 1899 and withdrawn in October 1956, the month after this picture was taken

23.9.56

The D20 class were familiar in the Hull area for a great many years – no. 62372 was photographed at Hull Dairycoates depot. Note the word 'store' chalked on the buffer. As with many members of the class it was probably used around this time on specials or holiday excursions. No. 62372 completed fifty years in service being built in October 1906 and withdrawn in November 1956

23.9.56

D30 class 4–4–0 3P

Designer: W.P. Reid. Introduced in 1914 for the North British Railway.

Principal dimensions

Weight:	Locomotive	57 tons 16 cwt
	Tender	46 tons 13 cwt
Boiler pressure:		165 lb/sq in
Driving wheels:		6 ft 6 in
Tractive effort:		18,700 lb
Cylinders:		(2) 20 in x 26 in

Stephenson valve gear – piston valves.

All of the twenty-four locomotives of this class that remained in service in 1955 were D30/2, carrying names from Sir Walter Scott's novels:

62418	*The Pirate*	62430	*Jingling Geordie*
62419	*Meg Dods*	62431	*Kenilworth*
62420	*Dominie Sampson*	62432	*Quentin Durward*
62421	*Laird o' Monkbarns*	62434	*Kettledrummie*
62422	*Caleb Balderstone*	62435	*Norna*
62423	*Dugald Dalgetty*	62436	*Lord Glenvarloch*
62424	*Calverhouse*	62437	*Adam Woodcock*
62425	*Ellangowan*	62438	*Peter Poundtext*
62426	*Cuddie Headrigg*	62439	*Father Ambrose*
62427	*Dumbledykes*	62440	*Wandering Willie*
62428	*The Talisman*	62441	*Black Duncan*
62429	*The Abbot*	62442	*Simon Glover*

The D30/2s were built at Cowlairs works, fifteen in 1914 and a further five being added in 1915 and again in 1930. One D30/2 was withdrawn in 1947.

During the mid-fifties locomotives of this class were to be found at several Scottish depots. Among their duties were cross-country services and local passenger trains. General withdrawals started in 1957 and eight were withdrawn between 1958 and 1959. Following the massive inroads that had been made into the class, only two were still in service in 1960, both of which were withdrawn in June. Unfortunately none have been preserved.

The D30 class was very familiar in the Edinburgh area, despite the depot at St Margaret's having only two in its allocation. Several locomotives of this class were usually to be found there, having worked their way in from other depots. No. 62421 *Laird o' Monkbarns* was a St Margaret's engine, and when this picture was taken it had recently received the attention of cleaners. The D30 names were painted on the leading splasher

21.8.55

Many pre-grouping locomotives were still receiving a general overhaul in the mid-fifties. No. 62430 *Jingling Geordie* had recently returned from what was to be its last works visit when photographed at Thornton. In less than two years it was withdrawn and cut up at Inverurie works in March 1957

23.8.55

Thornton depot was an excellent location to find both D30s and D34s in the mid-fifties. No. 62419 *Meg Dods* was a Thornton engine and was awaiting its next duty. This locomotive was among the batch withdrawn in 1957, ending its days at Inverurie works in October of that year

23.8.55

D34 class 4–4–0 3P 'Glens'

Designer: W.P. Reid. Introduced in 1913 for the North British Railway.
Total built: 32.

Principal dimensions

Weight:	Locomotive	57 tons 4 cwt
	Tender	46 tons 13 cwt
Boiler pressure:		165 lb/sq in
Driving wheels:		6 ft 0 in
Tractive effort:		20,260 lb
Cylinders:		(2) 20 in x 26 in

Stephenson valve gear – piston valves.

Thirty survived to be taken over by British Railways. In 1955 twenty-seven, numbered 62467–62498, remained in service, listed below. All members of the class carried the names of Scottish glens:

62467	*Glenfinnan*		62484	*Glen Lyon*
62468	*Glen Orchy*		62485	*Glen Murran*
62469	*Glen Douglas*		62487	*Glen Arklet*
62470	*Glen Roy*		62488	*Glen Aladale*
62471	*Glen Falloch*		62489	*Glen Dessary*
62472	*Glen Nevis*		62490	*Glen Fintaig*
62474	*Glen Croe*		62492	*Glen Garvin*
62475	*Glen Beasdale*		62493	*Glen Gloy*
62477	*Glen Dochart*		62494	*Glen Gour*
62478	*Glen Quoich*		62495	*Glen Luss*
62479	*Glen Sheil*		62496	*Glen Loy*
62480	*Glen Fruin*		62497	*Glen Mallie*
62482	*Glen Mamie*		62498	*Glen Moidart*
62483	*Glen Garry*			

Withdrawals commenced again in 1958 and continued steadily until by 1961 only five survived, these at widely scattered depots in the Scottish region. The last survivor was no. 62496 *Glen Loy* which was withdrawn in December 1961, still allocated to Eastfield. After ten months storage at Bo'ness it was cut up by Connells of Calder in September 1962. One member of the class has survived, no. 62469 *Glen Douglas*, built in September 1913.

The 'Glens' will be best remembered for their work on the difficult West Highland line, especially during the LNER days. By the fifties they were to be found at many Scottish depots, including those in the north of Scotland.

No. 62468 *Glen Orchy* receiving repairs at its home depot Thornton. This was the second member of the class to be built, being completed in September 1913. It remained at Thornton until withdrawn in September 1958, when it was despatched north to Inverurie works, where it was cut up in October 1959

23.8.55

The last member of the 'Glen' class to remain in service was No. 62496 *Glen Loy*, seen here with overflowing tender at Eastfield, its home depot. The locomotive had recently received a general overhaul and was in splendid condition. No. 62496 remained at Eastfield until withdrawn in December 1961, ending its days in a scrapyard at Calder

26.8.55

D16 class 4–4–0 3P

By 1955 all the D16s remaining in service were D16/3s introduced in 1933, rebuilds of earlier D15 and D16/2 locomotives. These engines were widely known as 'Clauds'. One example was named *Claud Hamilton* no. 62546 which was withdrawn in June 1957.
Designer: H.N. Gresley (D16/3 only).

Principal dimensions

Weight:	Locomotive	55 tons 18 cwt
	Tender	39 tons 5 cwt
Boiler pressure:		180 lb/sq in
Driving wheels:		7 ft 0 in
Tractive effort:		17,095 lb
Cylinders:		(2) 19 in x 26 in

The D16s were at one time responsible for the majority of the expresses in East Anglia. Even in the fifties they were mostly still employed on passenger work, although they could also frequently be seen on parcels and fast goods workings. In the mid-fifties they could be found hard at work in many areas: Lincoln-based engines working through to Derby, Peterborough engines to the Midlands, and Cambridge engines appearing at Oxford. The last to be withdrawn was no. 62613 of March depot in October 1960. Most of the class, including the last survivor, ended their days at Stratford works. None survive.

Many D16s were often seen with slight damage to the front buffer beam, as was the case with no. 62557 at Cambridge, one of the sizeable number of this class allocated to the depot. This D16/3 was one still retaining the original footplating and slide valves after rebuilding

3.4.55

This picture shows clearly the modified footplating of no. 62513. The engine was rebuilt from D15 class in September 1942, remaining in service until November 1958, completing a very commendable fifty-seven years. The rebuild also included a larger round-topped boiler. The first rebuilds to H.N. Gresley's instructions were in 1933

10.4.53

D11 class 4–4–0 3P 'Directors'

Designer: J.G. Robinson. Introduced in 1919 for the Great Central Railway and known as 'Large Directors', being a development of an earlier 4–4–0 design.
Total built: 35.

Principal dimensions

Weight:	Locomotive	61 tons 3 cwt
	Tender	48 tons 6 cwt
Boiler pressure:		180 lb/sq in
Driving wheels:		6 ft 9 in
Tractive effort:		19,645 lb
Cylinders:		(2) 20 in x 26 in

Stephenson valve gear – piston valves.

The D11s were built in two batches: eleven at Gorton works between 1919 and 1922, classified D11/1; and a further twenty-four in 1924 by Kitson & Co. of Leeds and Armstrong Whitworth & Co., each building twelve. These became known as 'Scottish Directors' as they were built to the Scottish loading gauge; they were listed as D11/2. All the D11s carried names. Those built for Scottish service had names originating from the works of Sir Walter Scott, some of which sounded strange to enthusiasts from south of the border.

All the D11s were taken over by British Railways and allocated nos. 62660–94. One example has been preserved, no. 62660 *Butler-Henderson*, now part of the National Collection in York.

62660	*Butler-Henderson*	62678	*Luckie Mucklebackit*
62661	*Gerard Powys Dewhurst*	62679	*Lord Glenallan*
62662	*Prince of Wales*	62680	*Lucy Ashton*
62663	*Prince Albert*	62681	*Captain Craigengelt*
62664	*Princess Mary*	62682	*Haystoun of Bucklaw*
62665	*Mons*	62683	*Hobbie Elliott*
62666	*Zeebrugge*	62684	*Wizard of the Moor*
62667	*Somme*	62685	*Malcolm Graeme*
62668	*Jutland*	62686	*The Fiery Cross*
62669	*Ypres*	62687	*Lord James of Douglas*
62670	*Marne*	62688	*Ellen Douglas*
62671	*Bailie MacWheeble*	62689	*Maid of Lorn*
62672	*Baron of Bradwardine*	62690	*The Lady of the Lake*
62673	*Evan Dhu*	62691	*Laird of Balmawhapple*
62674	*Flora MacIvor*	62692	*Allan-Bane*
62675	*Colonel Gardiner*	62693	*Roderick Dhu*
62676	*Jonathan Oldbuck*	62694	*James Fitzjames*
62677	*Edie Ochiltree*		

By the 1950s the D11s in England were mostly reduced to cross-country workings, with some examples spending time stored. Those based at Lincoln worked services to Nottingham and Derby. In Scotland D11s were to be found at a number of depots, Haymarket (Edinburgh) and Eastfield (Glasgow) having most in the early fifties. Towards the end of the decade some were withdrawn while others spent considerable periods lying out of use or stored. The last of the D11/1s to be withdrawn was no. 62666 *Zeebrugge* in December 1960. The Scottish engines lasted slightly longer, with no. 62685 *Malcolm Graeme* being condemned in January 1962.

Prior to the war the 'Directors' were often seen on the East Coast Main Line on principal expresses. During the fifties their main duties were cross-country traffic, although on at least one occasion a 'Director' is known to have worked south of Peterborough.

Several 'Directors' were allocated to Lincoln depot during the fifties, working trains to Nottingham and Derby. Here no. 62660 *Butler-Henderson* coals up at Lincoln St Marks depot (a sub-shed to 40A Lincoln). Alongside is *Compound* no. 40935 which also worked these services. *Butler-Henderson* was withdrawn in October 1960 and is preserved as part of the National Collection in York

14.8.55

A number of 'Directors' spent long periods in store at Trafford Park depot. Here no. 62668 *Jutland* is pictured among them. The smokebox door is wide open and the tender is partially coaled up. No. 62668 did work again on a limited number of occasions in the Sheffield area. Withdrawal was in November 1960 and it was cut up at Doncaster works the same month

22.9.57

The narrow brass nameplate carried by D11/1 no. 62668 *Jutland*, named after the famous First World War naval battle

The sole surviving 'Director' no. 62660 *Butler-Henderson* in action on the Great Central Railway at Loughborough, restored to lined BR livery shortly before returning to the National Railway Museum at York

22.2.92

The D11s built in 1924 were constructed to the Scottish loading gauge. No. 62684 *Wizard of the Moor* was photographed leaving Eastfield shed. The locomotive was one of the twelve built by Armstrong Whitworth & Co. in 1924; withdrawal from service was in October 1959

26.8.55

Busy times at Thornton depot, with two very different 4–4–0 designs receiving attention at the ash-pits. No. 62671 *Bailie MacWheeble* had just worked in from Glasgow. Alongside is D49 'Shire' class no. 62704 *Stirlingshire*, a Thornton engine

23.8.55

D49 class 4–4–0 3P 'Shires' and 'Hunts'

Introduced by H.N. Gresley in 1927 these locomotives were an invaluable LNER design for use on secondary lines or intermediate duties in the North-East and Scotland. Two versions of the class existed: D49/1 with piston valves and D49/2 with Lentz Rotary Cam poppet valves. One further locomotive no. 62768, was rebuilt in 1942 with two inside cylinders and Stephenson motion and piston valves (withdrawn 1952).

In all a total of seventy-six D49s were built at Darlington between 1927 and 1935. All were taken into BR stock.

Designer: H.N. Gresley.
Total built: 76.

Principal dimensions

Weight:	Locomotive	62–6 tons
	Tender	44 tons 2 cwt
Boiler pressure:		180 lb/sq in
Driving wheels:		6 ft 8 in
Tractive effort:		21,555 lb

62700	*Yorkshire*		62729	*Rutlandshire*
62701	*Derbyshire*		62730	*Berkshire*
62702	*Oxfordshire*		62731	*Selkirkshire*
62703	*Hertfordshire*		62732	*Dumfries-shire*
62704	*Stirlingshire*		62733	*Northumberland*
62705	*Lanarkshire*		62734	*Cumberland*
62706	*Forfarshire*		62735	*Westmorland*
62707	*Lancashire*		62736	*The Bramham Moor*
62708	*Argyllshire*		62737	*The York and Ainsty*
62709	*Berwickshire*		62738	*The Zetland*
62710	*Lincolnshire*		62739	*The Badsworth*
62711	*Dunbartonshire*		62740	*The Bedale*
62712	*Morayshire*		62741	*The Blankney*
62713	*Aberdeenshire*		62742	*The Braes of Derwent*
62714	*Perthshire*		62743	*The Cleveland*
62715	*Roxburghshire*		62744	*The Holderness*
62716	*Kincardineshire*		62745	*The Hurworth*
62717	*Banffshire*		62746	*The Middleton*
62718	*Kinross-shire*		62747	*The Percy*
62719	*Peebles-shire*		62748	*The Southwold*
62720	*Cambridgeshire*		62749	*The Cottesmore*
62721	*Warwickshire*		62750	*The Pytchley*
62722	*Huntingdonshire*		62751	*The Albrighton*
62723	*Nottinghamshire*		62752	*The Atherstone*
62724	*Bedfordshire*		62753	*The Belvoir*
62725	*Inverness-shire*		62754	*The Berkeley*
62726	*The Meynell*		62755	*The Bilsdale*
62727	*The Quorn*		62756	*The Brocklesby*
62728	*Cheshire*		62757	*The Burton*

62758	The Cattistock		62767	The Grove
62759	The Craven		62768	The Morpeth
62760	The Cotswold		62769	The Oakley
62761	The Derwent		62770	The Puckeridge
62762	The Fernie		62771	The Rufford
62763	The Fitzwilliam		62772	The Sinnington
62764	The Garth		62773	The South Durham
62765	The Goathland		62774	The Staintondale
62766	The Grafton		62775	The Tynedale

In 1955 all were still in the North Eastern and Scottish regions, allocated to many depots. The arrival on the scene of diesel multiple units and line closures affected many of their duties. Withdrawals commenced in September 1957 when no. 62713 *Aberdeenshire* was condemned at Thornton. Thereafter withdrawals increased steadily until the last survivor, no. 62712 *Morayshire*, was withdrawn at Hawick in July 1961. Fortunately it was not the end of the road for this locomotive as it was purchased for preservation and is now on the Bo'ness and Kinneil Railway.

One of the D49/1s allocated to the Scottish region was no. 62721 *Warwickshire*, seen here at St Margaret's depot (Edinburgh). This engine was among the first to go, being withdrawn from St Margaret's in August 1958 after making its final journey to Darlington works where it ended its days the same month

21.8.55

No. 62701 *Derbyshire* was completed at Darlington works in November 1927. When photographed it was at Hull Botanic Garden shed. This engine was a D49/1 with piston valves and was running with a rebuilt GC tender

23.9.56

No. 62737 *The York and Ainsty,* an example of the D49/2 with Lenz rotary cam poppet valves, was photographed at Darlington. This engine was withdrawn in January 1958 from Hull Botanic Gardens depot, ending its days at Darlington's scrap road one month later

8.7.56

The nameplate of 'Hunt' class D49/2 no. 62737 *The York and Ainsty*. Note the fox emblem carried on the nameplates; note also the work's plate, this having received a screw-on inset carrying the locomotive's BR number

This picture conveys the short wheelbase of these very useful 4–4–0s. No. 62772 *The Sinnington* was photographed at Selby. It was one of the last batch of locomotives built in 1935 with a new straight-sided tender and piston valves

23.9.56

E4 class 2–4–0 1MT

Designer: J. Holden for the Great Eastern Railway.
Total buit: 100, 1891–1902.
At the end of 1955 ten of these study locomotives still remained in service. These were the last examples of the 2–4–0 wheel arrangement in regular service on British Railways. The three Midland and South Western Junction Railway locomotives built in 1894 became extinct in 1954. Numbered 62780–62797.

Principal dimensions

Weight:	Locomotive	40 tons 6 cwt
	Tender	30 tons 13 cwt
Boiler pressure:		160 lb/sq in
Driving wheels:		5ft 8in
Tractive effort:		14,700
Cylinders:		(2) 17½ in x 24 in

Stephenson motion – slide valves.

Several E4s were fitted with side-window cabs for working over the exposed and difficult Stainmore–Penrith line. Three of the engines were among the 1956 survivors.

Cambridge had a long association with the class. From here the locomotives' duties took them to Mildenhall and Huntingdon. Most strenuous of all was the Colchester service, where the engines frequently handled six- or seven-coach trains on this difficult cross-country route.

The last survivor was no. 62785. This engine spent some time allocated to Hitchin depot where it was used on occasions on the RAF Henlow leave trains. This locomotive still survives today, part of the National Collection, resplendent in its Great Eastern blue livery, and still in former Great Eastern Railway territory at Bressingham Steam Museum.

When this picture of no. 62785 was taken at Hitchin, it was the last survivor of the class. At the time the E4 and a J15, no. 65479, were used to work the RAF Henlow leave trains over the Midland Railway Bedford branch (long since lifted). This locomotive still survives today and is to be seen at Bressingham Steam Museum restored to Great Eastern blue livery

14.10.56

During the mid-fifties Cambridge placed some of its allocation of E4s in store. Carefully greasing the moving parts and placing tarpaulin sheets over the chimneys, several of these E4s were later returned to traffic. No. 62786, seen here with its tender fully coaled, was withdrawn in July 1956

3.4.55

This E4 was one of those to receive side-window cabs, working the Darlington–Penrith trains over Stainmore. No. 62793 was on Stratford works' scrap line when photographed, having been withdrawn from Norwich depot in January 1955

7.5.55

Q6 class 0–8–0 6F

Designer: V. Raven for the North Eastern Railway.
Total built: 120 by Darlington works (70) and Armstrong Whitworth (50), 1919–21.
Introduced in 1913. Numbered 63340–63459.

Principal dimensions

Weight:	Locomotive	65 tons 18 cwt
	Tender	44 tons 2 cwt
Boiler pressure:		180 lb/sq in
Driving wheels:		4 ft 7½ in
Tractive effort:		28,800 lb
Cylinders:		(2) 20 in x 26 in

Stephenson motion.

These locomotives were among the workhorses of the North Eastern region, with duties comprising coal and other mineral traffic, together with general heavy goods trains.

During the mid-fifties the majority of the class were concentrated at depots in the Newcastle and Middlesbrough areas. A few examples were to be found at Selby and two at Leeds (Neville Hill). The class remained intact until May 1960 when no. 63372 was withdrawn. In 1963 withdrawals commenced in earnest; however, the last survivors remained in service for another four years. One of these, no. 63395, was purchased in 1967 by the North Eastern Locomotive Preservation group. This engine has now been on the North Yorkshire Moors Railway for many years.

During their working life the Q6s were not fitted with vacuum brakes, although these have been fitted to the Q6 in preservation, which enables it to be used on passenger trains.

There was generally very little variation among the Q6s in later years, except in the case of tenders, some engines running with those from withdrawn locomotives that had been found to be in better condition.

The 150th anniversary celebrations of the Stockton and Darlington Railway held at Shildon in August 1975 will be long remembered. Many famous engines took part, including the magnificently restored Q6 2238 (no. 63395) built in 1918 and preserved by the North Yorkshire Moors Railway.

No. 63427 had just arrived at Consett shed, already having been coaled and watered ready for its next duty. This engine was one of the batch of fifty built by Armstrongs in April 1920. No. 63427 remained in service until 1967

7.7.56

This picture of no. 63421 gives an idea of the boiler length of the Q6 class. Note the tiny works' plate above the second set of wheels from the cab end. Photographed at West Hartlepool depot, houses can be seen in the background; this was often the case near many motive power depots

7.7.56

No. 63377 stands in the shed yard at Consett depot. At weekends quite a number of Q6s could be found here during the fifties. In the background, part of an industrial complex can be seen, this providing much work for the ex-North Eastern 0–8–0s and 0–6–0s in the area

7.7.56

Q7 class 0–8–0 7F

Designer: V. Raven for the North Eastern Railway.
Total built: 15 by Darlington works in two batches: 5 in 1919, the remaining 10 in 1924.
Introduced in 1919. Numbered 63460–63474.

Principal dimensions

Weight:	Locomotive	71 tons 12 cwt
	Tender	44 tons 2 cwt
Boiler pressure:		180 lb/sq in
Driving wheels:		4 ft 7¼ in
Tractive effort:		36,963 lb
Cylinders:		(3) 18½ in x 26 in

Stephenson motion – 8¾ in piston valves.

All the engines survived to nationalization. The withdrawal of the entire class was in late 1962; one example is preserved.

These powerful three-cylinder freight locomotives were introduced only a few years after the highly successful Q6 class. All members of the class were to be found in the North-East. Shortly after the first example went into service and had been suitably run in, the opportunity was taken to carry out Dynamometer car tests, which soon proved the design to be very powerful.

Five were fitted with twin Westinghouse air pumps. While the class had previously been working the Tyne Dock–Consett iron ore trains, the introduction of new large capacity hopper wagons in 1951, with doors operating on compressed air, made these fittings necessary. The Q7s were later joined by 01s, modified in this way. Eventually the Q7s handed over these duties to Standard 9F 2–10–0s.

The class remained intact until late 1962 with two being withdrawn in November of that year. The following month all thirteen remaining were condemned. Fortunately one, no. 63460, had been scheduled for preservation in the National Collection. After a period at Darlington the Q7 commenced its journey around the country, as did several other locomotives destined for preservation. The Q7 spent time stored at Stratford, Brighton and Hellifield, eventually finding its way to York. This fine locomotive was then loaned to the North Eastern Locomotive Preservation Group, joining the preserved Q6 at the North Yorkshire Moors Railway. Since restoration it has worked a great many passenger trains over this railway, the sharp gradients presenting no problem to the fine locomotive.

This is now the sole surviving member of the class, no. 63460, photographed at Tyne Dock shed. This locomotive was completed at Darlington in October 1919, remaining in service until 1962. It was fitted with Westinghouse pumps and vacuum brakes. Note the plain chimney fitted

7.7.56

No. 63463 awaiting repair at Tyne Dock shed, already minus a tender. This Q7 was one of the five class members fitted with twin Westinghouse pumps for working the Tyne Dock–Consett iron ore trains. The pump and air reservoir can be seen immediately in front of the cab. Note also the chimney with capuchon

7.7.56

In the mid-fifties no. 63464 was allocated to Blaydon depot, where this picture was taken. This locomotive is one with a steam brake only; note the three link couplings. The engine was also fitted with a different chimney

8.7.56

Another Q7 in trouble. No. 63467, a Tyne Dock engine, was receiving attention at Darlington depot. One set of driving wheels had been removed. The locomotive also shows signs of hard work, judging by the smokebox door. It was another example of those engines with a steam brake only

7.7.56

O4 class 2–8–0 7F

Designer: J.G. Robinson.

Principal dimensions

Weight:	Locomotive	
	range	72–4 tons
	Tender	48 tons 6 cwt
Boiler pressure:		180 lb/sq in
Driving wheels:		4 ft 8 in
Tractive effort:		31,325 lb
Cylinders:		(2) 21 in x 26 in

Stephenson motion – piston valves.

This class can justifiably be called one of the most important designs to have run on British Railways. Built in large quantities the O4 was to be seen in no less than seven different varieties. The last (O4/8) was introduced in 1944 and consisted of engines rebuilt with a 100A (B1-type) boiler still retaining the original cylinders.

The first O4 made its appearance from Gorton works in September 1911, to the design of J.G. Robinson, for the Great Central Railway. Several private builders were to construct locomotives of this type over the years namely: Kitson & Co., North British Locomotive Co., Nasmyth Wilson and R. Stephenson & Co.

The design was also chosen by the Government Railway Operating Division for military purposes during the First World War. Locomotives of this order were purchased by the LNER in 1924. Such was the suitability of the design that many of these engines

79

were sent overseas during the Second World War. Some were eventually to find themselves as far away as Australia, where, incidentally, three still survive today.

In spite of the many rebuildings and modifications over the years, quite a number of engines survived in their original form right up until being withdrawn from service.

British Railways took over 278 O4s in January 1948, plus many other locomotives, at one time members of this class, which had already been rebuilt to O1 specifications. The number series of the O4s and incorporating the O1s was nos. 63570–920.

In 1952 the government purchased five O4s and despatched them to the Suez War Department depot. These engines never returned home and were taken over by Egyptian State Railways.

The first O4 to be withdrawn was in December 1958, a Kitson & Co. locomotive, no. 63668. Thereafter inroads were made into the class. In one year (1962) no less than 108 were condemned. The last examples in service were withdrawn in 1966.

One O4 that survives in this country is no. 63601, an O4/1. This engine is part of the National Collection in York. It was withdrawn in June 1963.

This O4 was built by R. Stephenson & Co. and was one of those operated by the Railway Operating Division Royal Engineers, later to be taken over by the LNER. In this picture we see no. 63717 fresh from general overhaul approaching Peterborough. What is surprising is that when the next 'general' was due, the engine was rebuilt to class O4/8 with 100A (B1-type) boiler. After this it remained in service until it was withdrawn from Langwith Junction depot in April 1965, ending its days at Cashmores Great Bridge

24.9.55

No. 63597 pictured here at Tuxford depot was an O4/1, built by the North British Locomotive Co. in 1912. It was never rebuilt, having a small Belpaire boiler, steam and vacuum brakes and fitted with a water scoop. This engine remained in service until May 1961 and was cut up at Gorton works the following month

25.8.57

This O4 no. 63665 was one of the ex-Railway Operating Division locomotives, with steam brake only and no water scoop. Built by Kitson & Co. in 1918 it was classified O4/3 and withdrawn in December 1963. These ex-ROD locos were taken into LNER stock from 1924 onwards

Tuxford, 25.8.57

Another of the ex-ROD locomotives purchased by the LNER was no. 63714, photographed at Annesley. This engine had steam brake only and no water scoop. It remained in service at Darnall shed until March 1959; it was cut up at Gorton two months later

4.4.54

Photographed at Colwick while still an O4/3, no. 63877 was rebuilt to O4/8 in 1957. This engine was originally built by the North British Locomotive Co. in 1919; it was withdrawn in March 1965 and ended its days in a private contractor's scrapyard

This picture of no. 63727 was taken at Barnsley depot. Typical of the O4/1s this locomotive was built by Kitson & Co. in 1912. It was never rebuilt, retaining its Belpaire boiler to the end. It was withdrawn from Retford in February 1964 and cut up at Doncaster works

24.6.56

No. 63634, an example of the O4/7 design rebuilds introduced in 1939, with shortened O2-type boiler retaining GC smokebox. The locomotive was photographed at New England depot, note the old coaling stage in the background

13.3.55

No. 63615 was an O4/7, built at Gorton in 1914 as O4/1, and rebuilt to its present form, retaining the GC smokebox but with a shortened O2-type boiler, in 1939. It remained in service until September 1964

Mexborough depot, 24.6.56

This picture shows no. 63730 as an O4/3. It took on a different appearance in 1958 when it was rebuilt to O4/8 class, remaining in service until January 1966

Mexborough, 24.6.56

Newly rebuilt to class O4/8, no. 63718 was being shunted by an N5 at Barnsley depot. The engine was another of the ROD locomotives built by R. Stephenson & Co. in 1919. It was withdrawn from Retford in December 1962; after a period in storage it was cut up at Doncaster works

24.6.56

This photograph of no. 63695 was taken at Sheffield Darnall shed. This loco was an O4/3 taken over from the ROD. Built by R. Stephenson & Co. in 1918, it remained in service until December 1962

24.6.56

O1 class 2–8–0 8F

Designer: E. Thompson, 1944. Rebuilds of O4 class.
Total rebuilt: 58, 1944–9. Only seven were actually rebuilt after nationalization. All rebuilding was done at Gorton works.

Principal dimensions

Weight:	Locomotive	73 tons 6 cwt
	Tender (O4 type)	48 tons 6 cwt
Boiler pressure:		225 lb/sq in
Driving wheels:		4 ft 8 in
Tractive effort:		35,520 lb
Cylinders:		(2) 20 in x 26 in

Walschaerts valve gear – 10 in piston valves.

These locomotives were part of the LNER modernization programme. The design incorporated the Diagram 100A boiler as fitted to the B1s, and new cylinders. All were paired with Standard GC 4,000 gallon tenders.

Locomotives of class O1 were chosen for the BR Interchange Trials in 1948. These trials included the Western Region 28XX class, London Midland 8F, and ex-WD 2–8–0 and 2–10–0 designs. Four routes were chosen, the East Coast main line one being from New England–Ferme Park, London. The O1s were credited with the best coal consumption.

During the early fifties all the Eastern region's class O1s were to be found at Annesley depot. Among their principal duties were heavy goods traffic to Woodford. The other five engines were allocated to Tyne Dock: these were fitted with twin Westinghouse pumps for operating the wagons on the Consett–Tyne Dock iron ore trains.

In the late fifties some O1s were transferred to other depots, their duties being handed over to Standard 9F 2–10–0s. March shed received a considerable number of the class, some of which were to remain there until the depot closed. Several were at times stored in the shed yard in the company of other engines, including displaced 'Britannias' which were later transferred to London Midland region.

The remaining examples of the class soldiered on until July 1965 when the last eight were withdrawn.

It was originally intended that a total of one hundred and sixty O4 class 2–8–0s would be rebuilt to class O1. These would replace several other classes in service. However, only fifty-eight examples were rebuilt before the programme was cancelled in 1949.

March depot had quite a number of O1s in its allocation during the late fifties and early sixties. Included was no. 63687, seen here in the largely deserted shed yards. This particular locomotive was withdrawn in October 1963, after which it remained at March for three months awaiting disposal. Eventually it was towed to Doncaster works where it was cut up

9.9.62

Sundays would find most of Annesley's O1s in the shed. Here, three await their next duties. Prominent is no. 63777, which was to remain in service until November 1962. After being stored for nine months, it was cut up at Crewe works

4.4.54

O1 no. 63856, heading one of the Tyne Dock–Consett iron ore trains, passes Tyne Dock depot. Note the wagons, introduced in 1951, necessitating the locomotive to be fitted with twin Westinghouse pumps to operate the doors

7.7.56

This almost broadside view of no. 63872 was taken at March with the coaling tower in the background, a landmark for miles around in the Fenland landscape. This O1 was withdrawn in June 1964, ending its days with a scrap dealer in Sheffield

1963

A few years previously this area would have been packed with engines. March was a shadow of its former self when this picture was taken; most of those here are visitors. O1 no. 63746 was still operational from the depot. This engine moved to Staveley from where it was withdrawn in February 1964

28.7.63

No. 63784 had probably received works attention shortly before this photograph was taken, judging by the smokebox which had been repainted. This was often done on intermediate visits. Note the works plate below the number

Annesley depot, 4.4.54

O2 class 2–8–0 8F

Designer: H.N. Gresley. Introduced in 1918 for Great Northern Railway.
Total built: 67, by Doncaster works and North British Locomotive Co. Numbered 63922–63987.

Principal dimensions

Weight:	78 tons 13 cwt (with variations)
Boiler pressure:	180 lb/sq in
Driving wheels:	4 ft 8 in
Tractive effort:	36,470 lb
Cylinders:	(3) 18½ in x 26 in

Walschaerts valve gear with derived motion – 8 in piston valves.

This class was designed for handling heavy mineral traffic. The pioneer engine made its appearance from Doncaster works in 1918. It was another three years before the next ten were completed, this time by the North British Locomotive Co., all ten being finished in May of that year. Subsequent deliveries from 1923 onwards were all Doncaster-built locomotives.

Many of the locomotives were rebuilt to O2/4 specifications, these having 100A B1 (type) boilers and extended smokeboxes. Most of the class had side-window cabs. All sixty-seven locomotives were handed over to British Railways, the first to be withdrawn, the prototype engine, in May 1948. The class remained intact for twelve years, after which, in 1960, four were withdrawn. The final examples went in November 1963. None have survived into preservation.

During the fifties O2s were frequently seen on the East Coast main line north of Peterborough and at March. Although they were commonplace south of Peterborough in the thirties, after nationalization they were very rare on this section of line.

No. 63942, an example of an O2/2, built at Doncaster in 1924, and still retaining its original cab. The engine remained in service until September 1963, when a large number of the class were withdrawn. No. 63942 was cut up at Doncaster in February 1964

24.6.56

Judging from the appearance of no. 63951 the locomotive had recently been cleaned. The engine was an O2/3 built at Doncaster in 1932. The oval works plate can be seen on the side of the smokebox. This locomotive ended its days at Doncaster, being cut up in July 1962

23.9.56

Among the last examples of the class to be withdrawn was O2/4 no. 63924, which was condemned in November 1963. This locomotive is one which was rebuilt with a 100A boiler and extended smokebox, in this case still retaining a Great Northern tender

March, 13.3.55

91

Class O2/3 no. 63959 was built at Doncaster in January 1934. The part 3 design was introduced in 1932 having reduced boiler mountings. This locomotive was among the first to be withdrawn in October 1960; it was cut up two months later. Note the straight sided Group Standard tender
Doncaster, 25.8.57

No. 63923 ambles south along the East Coast main line at Walton near Peterborough with a heavy coal train. This locomotive was one of the batch built by the North British Locomotive Co. in 1921, receiving a side window cab in 1940. It was not rebuilt, remaining as an O2/1 until withdrawn in December 1962

24.9.55

J6 class 0–6–0 3F

Designer: H.N. Gresley. Introduced in 1911 for the Great Northern Railway.
Total built: 110 at Doncaster works, 1911–22. The entire class passed into British Railway stock, receiving the number series 64170–279.

Principal dimensions

Weight:	Locomotive	50 tons 10 cwt
	Tender	43 tons 2 cwt
Boiler pressure:		170 lb/sq in
Driving wheels:		5 ft 2 in
Tractive effort:		21,875 lb
Cylinders:		(2) 19 in x 26 in

Stephenson valve gear – piston valves.

During the fifties J6s allocated to New England depot were to be found shunting and on short trips, working at the many brickworks in the area. These were by no means the only duties allocated, as the engines appeared on local goods and engineers' trains. Locomotives of this class were also allocated to many other Eastern region depots.

When the first members of the class were withdrawn in 1955 others were still receiving general overhauls at Doncaster works. The last examples remained in service until June 1962.

Many J6s were employed on engineers' trains. No. 64197 of Hitchin depot was on such a duty just south of Huntingdon. This J6 was completed in May 1913 remaining in stock until October 1959
2.10.55

Bright as a new pin after a general overhaul at Doncaster works, no. 64267 only survived for two years after this picture was taken, being withdrawn in July 1958

24.6.54

This photograph of no. 64199 clearly shows the rather cramped and open footplate of a J6. No. 64199 was one of the first batch built, being completed at Doncaster in May 1913. It was withdrawn in May 1958

Colwick depot, 4.4.54

The J6 was widely distributed in the Eastern region. No. 64276 was one of three allocated to Leeds Copley Hill depot in the mid-fifties. Judging by the locomotive's appearance, it had not long been through the works when photographed at Ardsley. The typical large, brass, oval Doncaster builder's plate shows up clearly over the middle splasher

13.5.56

J11 class 0–6–0 3F

Designer: J.G. Robinson.
Total built: 175.

Principal dimensions

Weight:	51 tons 19 cwt (with variations)
Boiler pressure:	180 lb/sq in
Driving wheels:	5 ft 2 in
Tractive effort:	21,960–25,644 lb
Cylinders:	(2) (three variations) 18½ in x 26 in
	20 in x 26 in
	18 in x 26 in

Stephenson motion – some slide, others piston valves.

These were the first new goods locomotives designed by J.G. Robinson for the Great Central Railway. The pioneer of this 175-strong class made its appearance in September 1901, the first batch of forty engines being built by Neilson, Reed & Co. between 1901 and 1902.

95

Three other private builders Beyer, Peacock & Co., Vulcan Foundry and the Yorkshire Engine Co., also built J11s, as did Gorton works. Construction was between 1901 and 1910, 174 engines being taken over by British Railways and allocated number series 64280–453.

This class was latterly in two parts, J11 and J11/3. The newer models were engines rebuilt with long travel piston valves and higher pitched boilers.

From their earliest days these engines became known as 'Pom-Poms', a term still in use in their final years. This nickname originated from their crisp exhaust sounds, similar to a quick firing gun used in the Boer War.

The J11s were always popular with enginemen, and although primarily goods engines they were often used on passenger duties. The first J11 was withdrawn in 1954, but examples of the class remained in service until October 1962.

Eighteen of these engines saw service in France during the First World War. One member of the class would have been an ideal subject for preservation, but unfortunately this was not to be.

This immaculate J11, no. 64365, had recently received a general overhaul, almost certainly its last, when photographed at Sheffield Darnall depot. This engine was one of those built at Gorton works, being completed in July 1904 and remaining in service until August 1959

24.6.56

Another clean J11, this time no. 64403, pictured at Retford GC shed. During the fifties many of the J11s were in a rather shabby condition. This locomotive was a Gorton-built engine, completed in March 1907 and withdrawn in July 1960

25.8.57

J35 class 0–6–0 3F

Designer: W.P. Reid.
Total built: 76.
Introduced in 1906 by the North British Railway.

Principal dimensions

Weight:	Locomotive	50 tons 15 cwt
	Tender	37 tons 15 cwt
Boiler pressure:		180 lb/sq in
Driving wheels:		5 ft 0 in
Tractive effort:		22,080 lb
Cylinders:		(2) 18½ x 26 in

Seventy-six engines of the class were built, the majority of which were by the North British Locomotive Co., their Atlas, Queens Park and Hyde Park works all building batches. Thirty engines were also constructed at Cowlairs works. All except five members of the class came into BR ownership, receiving number series 64460–535.

The J35s remained intact for ten years after nationalization, when inroads were made into their numbers, six going in 1958 and twelve remaining in service until 1962, when the class became extinct.

There were two parts of the J35 class: part 4 had slide valve engines, while J35/5 had piston valves. All were superheated.

Fresh from overhaul at Inverurie works, no. 64463, a Hawick depot engine, was in the process of working its way home when photographed at Dundee. It was built by the North British Locomotive Co. at its Atlas works and remained in service until September 1960

23.8.55

No. 64532 was one of the last batch of J35s built at Cowlairs works in 1913. The engine is seen here with the more tapered type of chimney fitted to some members of the class. No. 64532 was photographed at Seafield depot, a sub-shed to St Margaret's. This was a J35/4 slide valve locomotive

21.8.55

J37 class 0–6–0 4F

Designer: W.P. Reid for the North British Railway. Introduced in 1914.
Total built: 104 by Cowlairs works and the North British Locomotive Co., 1914–21. This very useful class survived intact to become BR nos. 64536–639. These locomotives were a superheated development of the J35 introduced eight years earlier.

Principal dimensions

Weight:	Locomotive	54 tons 14 cwt
	Tender	40 tons 19 cwt
Boiler pressure:		180 lb/sq in
Driving wheels:		5 ft 0 in
Tractive effort:		25,210 lb
Cylinders:		(2) 19½ in x 26 in

Stephenson motion – piston valves.

During the fifties J37s were widespread in Scotland. Withdrawals commenced in 1959, but it was not until 1962–3 that the class started to be withdrawn in large numbers. The J37s were a sturdy design and highly popular with enginemen. Unfortunately none have survived into preservation.

The Scottish region depot of St Margaret's had a large number of J37s in its allocation. These were often to be found at the various sub-sheds within its control. No. 64606 was photographed at its home depot, showing signs of hard work on the base of its smokebox door. This particular J37 was built by the North British Locomotive Co. in 1919

21.8.55

J37 no. 64596 pictured at the busy Thornton depot in the fifties, the shed having an allocation of over 100 engines of many designs. This J37 was one of the batch built by the North British Locomotive Co. in 1919 at their Atlas works, remaining in service until April 1961. Note the J72 (North Eastern design) 0–6–0T in the background

23.8.55

J19 class 0–6–0 4F

Designer: S.D. Holden. Introduced in 1912 for the Great Eastern Railway.
Total built: 35.

Principal dimensions

Weight:	Locomotive	50 tons 7 cwt
	Tender	38 tons 5 cwt
Boiler pressure:		170 lb/sq in
Driving wheels:		4 ft 11 in
Tractive effort:		27,430 lb
Cylinders:		(2) 20 in x 26 in

Stephenson valve gear – piston valves.

Thirty-five locomotives were built in total, all at Stratford works, ten in 1912 as J18 class, later rebuilt to J19 class. A further twenty-five were built from 1916 to 1920. All survived to be taken into British Railways stock. Number series allocated 64640–74.

These locomotives underwent considerable modification over the years, including the fitting of new boilers of the same type as those fitted to the D16/3 ('Clauds'). During the fifties J19s were to be found at many of the principal depots in the Great Eastern section. Ten were allocated to March at one time: these were often employed on heavy goods traffic to London. The class remained intact until 1958 when no. 64645 was withdrawn.

The following two years saw massive inroads into these and the other ex-Great Eastern 0–6–0 classes. By 1962 only four locomotives remained in service, all of which were withdrawn during that year, rendering the class extinct.

Cambridge depot had three J19s in its allocation for a number of years, one of which was no. 64673, seen here in the shed yard. The boiler and chimney of the same type as fitted to the D16/3 'Clauds' can be clearly seen

3.4.55

No. 64650 blasts through St Ives on its way to March heading a long train of coal empties. This engine was the first built as a J19 class in 1916. The previous ten locomotives were originally class J18 and were rebuilt to this design. No. 64650 remained in service until October 1960

13.3.54

J20 class 0–6–0 6F

Designer: A.J. Hill. Introduced in 1920 for the Great Eastern Railway.
Total built: 25 at Stratford works, 1920–22. All were taken into British Railways stock and numbered 64675–99.

Principal dimensions

Weight:	Locomotive	54 tons 15 cwt
	Tender	38 tons 5 cwt
Boiler pressure:		180 lb/sq in
Driving wheels:		4 ft 11 in
Tractive effort:		29,045 lb
Cylinders:		(2) 20 in x 28 in

Stephenson valve gear – piston valves.

These were powerful locomotives which during their service were reboilered with B12/1-type round-topped boilers from 1943 onwards. The last to receive one of these was in 1956.

March depot had a long association with the class, J20s being among the last ex-Great Eastern locomotives to remain in service at the depot. The first engine to be withdrawn was no. 64688, which was condemned in January 1959; thereafter withdrawals took place at an ever-increasing rate. The last four survivors were withdrawn in September 1962. Unfortunately no examples have survived into preservation.

No. 64693 was completed at Stratford in December 1922. In this picture it is seen on what was unofficially known as 'Cambridge Dump' – sidings which on occasions contained stored or locomotives awaiting works or repairs. no. 64693 was withdrawn in August 1960

3.4.55

Examples of March depot's J20s and J17 0–6–0s await their fate. Although withdrawn, no. 64699 still has a full tender of coal, as can be seen near the J17, which would have been shovelled out by hand, before the engine commenced its last journey. This J20 was the last built, being completed at Stratford in January 1923. It was also one of the last four survivors, all of which were withdrawn in September 1962

9.9.62

J39 class 0–6–0 4F

Designer: H.N. Gresley. Introduced in 1926 for the LNER.
Total built: 289 mostly at Darlington works, except for twenty-eight which were built by Beyer, Peacock & Co. in 1935. Construction of the class was between 1926 and 1941. All were taken over by British Railways, receiving numbers 64700–988.

Principal dimensions

Weight:	Locomotive	57 tons 17 cwt
	Tender	44 tons 4 cwt
	(Several tender types were fitted to the J39s with different weights.)	
Boiler pressure:		180 lb/sq in
Driving wheels:		5 ft 2 in
Tractive effort:		26,655 lb
Cylinders:		(2) 20 in x 26 in

Stephenson valve gear – piston valves.

Initially the class consisted of three parts depending on the type of tender: J39/1 Standard 3,500 gallon tender; J39/2 Standard 4,200 gallon tender; J39/3, fitted with mostly ex-North Eastern tenders. During the early fifties this was discontinued, tender changes having become commonplace.

J39s were to be found on many duties: heavy goods, fast goods, parcels and passenger trains on occasions. The class was distributed over a wide area in Eastern, North Eastern and Scottish regions, although in the mid-fifties they were very rarely seen south of Peterborough. Withdrawals commenced between 1960 and 1962; unfortunately not one example of this very important LNER class has survived.

No. 64860 is seen here with the standard straight-sided tender. This locomotive, built at Darlington, was among the last survivors, being withdrawn in December 1962. The J39s with their 5 ft 2 in driving wheels were capable of a fair turn of speed

Selby depot, 23.9.56

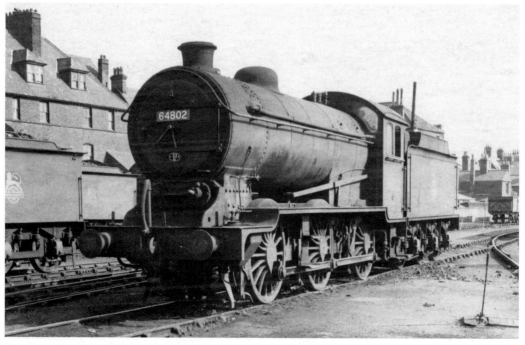

The majority of the J39 class were to be seen with the Standard 3,500 gallon tender. No. 64802 was photographed at Yarmouth Beach depot, being allocated at that time to Melton Constable. This locomotive was withdrawn in July 1960

18.8.57

This locomotive was an example of the J39/3, in this case running with an ex-North Eastern tender. No. 64972 was another of the Darlington-built engines which remained in service until December 1959

Annesley depot, 4.4.54

J39 no. 64719 ambles along the Leicester–Peterborough line near Walton with a mixed goods train. This class was principally employed on goods traffic, although it was to be seen on passenger trains on many occasions, especially during the summer months

24.9.55

J21 class 0–6–0 2F

Designer: T.W. Worsdell. Introduced in 1886.
Total built: 201 providing more powerful locomotives for the North Eastern Railway than those in service. Construction was at Gateshead and Darlington works. Most of the original engines were rebuilt except for the batch built in 1886 and the last between 1894 and 1895. Numbered 65033–65119.

Principal dimensions

Weight:	Locomotive	43 tons 15 cwt
	Tender	36 tons 19 cwt
Boiler pressure:		160 lb/sq in
Driving wheels:		5 ft 1¼ in
Tractive effort:		19,240 lb
Cylinders:		(2) 19 in x 24 in

Stephenson valve gear – piston valves.

Withdrawals from service of the class were very heavy during the thirties, only eighty-three remaining in service to be taken over by British Railways, who promptly condemned another large batch between 1948 and 1949. By the mid-fifties the class was getting thin on the ground, although examples could still be found at work at some depots.

The last to be withdrawn was no. 65033 in April 1962. This was the second withdrawal for this particular locomotive as it was one of eight that had been withdrawn in late 1939, only to be reinstated due to the onset of the Second World War. Consideration was given to saving a J21 no. 65033, and the sad remains of no. 65099 were to be seen at Darlington works for a long time, the latter engine being cut up. No. 65033 lives on in the North of England Open Air Museum, Beamish, not far from where it was built in 1889.

No. 65064 was still active at Darlington in 1956. This engine was completed at Gateshead works in October 1890 as a compound engine. In 1908 it was rebuilt as a 'simple' with piston valves; seven years later it was superheated. No. 65064 remained in service until September 1958

8.7.56

J21 no. 65070 was photographed at Blaydon – note the large spacious cabs fitted to these locomotives. This J21 was withdrawn in September 1960. The class was one of the most important introduced to the North Eastern Railway, with over 200 locomotives of the class eventually in service

8.7.56

J10 class 0–6–0 2F

Designer: H. Pollitt.
Total built: 84. Numbered 65126–65209.
The locomotives that remained in service in 1955 were all examples of the H. Pollitt development of earlier engines introduced in 1896 (J10/4 class), and the 1901 J.G. Robinson locomotives introduced in 1901 (classified J10/6). These were for the Manchester, Sheffield and Lincolnshire Railway and Great Central Railway respectively.

Principal dimensions

Weight:	Locomotive	41 tons 6 cwt
	Tender	37 tons 6 cwt (J10/6)
		43 tons (J10/4)
Boiler pressure:		160 lb/sq in
Driving wheels:		5 ft 1 in
Tractive effort:		18,780 lb
Cylinders:		(2) 18 in x 26 in

Stephenson motion – slide valves.

The J10s which remained in 1955 had been built by Beyer, Peacock & Co. and at Gorton works. Withdrawals of earlier engines had taken place in considerable numbers by the time BR came into existence; however, a total of seventy-eight were still in service at that time. Withdrawals took place at an ever-increasing pace throughout the fifties, until the last survivors, nos. 65157/98, were withdrawn in August 1961.

No. 65134, seen here at Northwich depot, was one of the engines built by Beyer, Peacock & Co. in 1896, classified J10/4. This locomotive remained in service until December 1959

22.9.57

Another example of the J10/4 class was no. 65153, seen about to refill its tender at Trafford Park depot. This was another of the locomotives built by Beyer, Peacock & Co. in 1896. It had only just over a year left in service when this picture was taken, being withdrawn in December 1956

16.10.55

No. 65181 is an example of the J10/6 built at Gorton works in June 1901. Note the spectacle plate fitted to the tender of this engine when photographed at Trafford Park depot. No. 65181 was one of the batch withdrawn in December 1956

16.10.55

J36 class 0–6–0 2F

Designer: M. Holmes for the North British Railway. Introduced in 1888.
Total built: 168 by Cowlairs works, Neilson & Co. and Sharp, Stewart & Co. between 1888 and 1900. Despite their age no less than 123 made it into BR service, many of these surviving into the sixties. In BR service they were allocated nos. 65210–346.

Principal dimensions

Weight:	Locomotive	41 tons 19 cwt
	Tender	33 tons 9 cwt
Boiler pressure:		165 lb/sq in
Driving wheels:		5 ft 0 in
Tractive effort:		19,690 lb
Cylinders:		(2) 18 in x 26 in

Stephenson motion – slide valves.

Engines of this class were used in France during the 1914–18 war. As recognition of the service these locomotives performed, a number were named, names being painted on the splasher. A few of these named locomotives were still in service during 1955, although some were no longer carrying their names. Those still in service were:

65216	*Byng*		65235	*Gough*
65217	*French*		65236	*Horne*
65222	*Somme*		65243	*Maude*
65223	*Plumer*		65253	*Joffre*
65224	*Mons*		65268	*Allenby*

Of these, 65243 *Maude*, built by Neilson & Co. in 1891, has been preserved at the Bo'ness and Kinneil Railway, the sole remaining example of the J36 class.

No. 65253 carried the name *Joffre*, although in this case it had been removed during a works visit. The names were painted on the splashers. No. 65253 was photographed at Dunfermline depot. Built in 1892 by Sharp, Stewart & Co. this engine remained in service until May 1963, a very creditable seventy-one years, including service overseas

23.8.55

The J36 class was to be found at many depots. No. 65339 was an Eastfield (Glasgow) engine, photographed leaving its home depot for its next duty. This J36 was one of the last batch built at Cowlairs works and was completed in July 1900. It remained in service until March 1961

26.8.55

J15 class 0–6–0 2F

Designer: T.W. Worsdell for the Great Eastern Railway. Introduced in 1883 as class Y14. *Total built*: 289, 1883–1913. Numbered 65356–65479.

Principal dimensions

Weight:	Locomotive	37 tons 2 cwt
	Tender	30 tons 13 cwt
Boiler pressure:		160 lb/sq in
Driving wheels:		4 ft 11 in
Tractive effort:		16,940 lb
Cylinders:		(2) 17½ in x 24 in

Stephenson valve gear – slide valves.

The first locomotive of the class was withdrawn way back in 1920. No less than forty-two years were to elapse before the last examples were withdrawn (nos. 65361, 65460/2/4/5/76 in September 1962.) One survives: no. 65462, at present on the North Norfolk Railway.

This sturdy 0–6–0 class was introduced by the Great Eastern mainly for goods traffic, although the engines frequently found themselves on passenger trains, specials and excursion traffic, as well as on many branch line services. During the First World War forty-three saw service in France and Belgium. All were eventually returned to this country. After overhaul they were reinstated with one exception: this engine, which had been badly damaged, was withdrawn. In the mid-fifties J15s were to be found at a number of sheds throughout East Anglia. One exception was no. 65479, which was allocated to Hitchin depot where it worked RAF Henlow leave trains over the branch to Hitchin.

Records exist of these locomotives even working express trains! One such occasion was in February 1955 when no. 65451 took over a heavy southbound express at Huntingdon from a failed 'Pacific'. The main line enginemen worked the struggling J15 as far as St Neots, where a V2 2–6–2 which had been commandeered from a goods train, took over. While heavy expresses were certainly out of their league these 0–6–0s were powerful for their size and capable of moving quite heavy loads. Over the years they performed many Herculean tasks, some of which I have witnessed personally.

The J15 class was to gain the record for construction of a locomotive in 1891 when Stratford works erected and steamed a J15 in just nine hours forty-seven minutes. In the process it gained the record from the London and North Western, who built a Webb 0–6–0 taking fifteen hours and thirty-three minutes longer.

During the early fifties the line between Huntingdon and St Ives witnessed the return of an afternoon goods train headed by a J15. Often these trains consisted of many wagons for forwarding on the East Coast main line. Here no. 65474 arrives back at Huntingdon East. The first wagon was loaded with agricultural machinery. This line was closed and completely lifted many years ago; where this picture was taken is now part of a busy bypass

16.3.54

Cambridge depot had an allocation of several J15s. One of their duties was the first Cambridge–Kettering train, the locomotive (usually no. 65390) remaining on LMR territory and returning home with the last train of the day. Another duty was the 'Huntingdon Pilot': this was on a ten-day rota basis. No. 65451 is seen here in Huntingdon yards. This locomotive remained in service until September 1959

15.6.55

Many of the J15s ran with stovepipe chimneys. No. 65454, photographed at Stratford, would appear to have been running with a patched-up example. This J15 remained in service until May 1959, completing fifty-three years service. Fortunately one locomotive of this remarkable class survives

7.5.55

The majority of J15s were fitted with steam brake only. No. 65356, seen here at March depot, was one of these locomotives, although in this case it had been fitted with a vacuum ejector. Built in 1888 no. 65356 remained in service until April 1957: the J15s were certainly long lived

13.5.55

No. 65461 had just crossed the wooden trestle bridge over the River Ouse, on its way to Huntingdon. This scene has many important features. The line itself, single at the time this picture was taken, has long since gone. The Hosiery Mill seen in the left background still working, is now converted to private dwellings. The mill (behind loco tender) has long since been demolished

10.8.54

J17 class 0–6–0 4F

Designer: J. Holden. Introduced in 1901 for the Great Eastern Railway.
Total built: 90.
These sturdy engines were originally designed for use on heavy goods traffic. The earlier engines were class J16 and later rebuilt. One locomotive was withdrawn as a result of enemy action in 1944; otherwise the class came over complete to BR ownership receiving nos. 65500–89.

There was some variation within the class: a number were fitted with vacuum ejectors, some had small tenders and a few ran with tender weatherboards.

Principal dimensions

Weight:	Locomotive	45 tons 8 cwt
	Tender	38 tons 2 cwt
Boiler pressure:		180 lb/sq in
Driving wheels:		4 ft 11 in
Tractive effort:		24,340 lb
Cylinders:		(2) 19 in x 26 in

Stephenson motion – slide valves.

During the fifties J17s were to be found at many East Anglian sheds, also at Stratford. As with several other 0–6–0 classes withdrawals commenced in 1954, the last example remaining in service until 1962. One engine has been preserved, no. 65567, now restored as LNER 1217E. This Stratford-built locomotive was completed in May 1905 and is now at The National Railway Museum, York.

No. 65511 was a typical example of the steam brake J17s, seen here at Stratford. This locomotive was originally built as a J16 at Stratford in November 1900; rebuilt in 1923 it remained in service until November 1960

7.5.55

This March depot J17 was one of those fitted with a vacuum ejector. No. 65562 was used on several rail enthusiasts' specials in its last years. The locomotive was on such a duty at Whittlesea when this photograph was taken, ready to work a 'special', comprised of open wagons, over the Benwick branch

9.9.56

This J17 no. 65508 was one of those running with small tenders, in this case also with a weatherboard. No. 65508 was a steam brake engine allocated to Stratford where this picture was taken. The locomotive was withdrawn from service in June 1958

7.5.55

J25 class 0–6–0 3F

Designer: W. Worsdell for the North Eastern Railway.
Total built: 120, construction taking place at Gateshead and Darlington works 1898–1902. Numbered 65645–65728.

Principal dimensions

Weight:	Locomotive (some variations – those quoted are for the majority in service in 1955) 39 tons 11 cwt
	Tender 36 tons 19 cwt
Boiler pressure:	160 lb/sq in
Driving wheels:	4 ft 7¼ in
Tractive effort:	21,905 lb
Cylinders:	(2) 18½ in x 26 in

Stephenson motion.

Withdrawals of this class commenced about the same time as the J21 0–6–0s, in the early thirties. Only seventy-six remained in service when taken over by British Railways. Here again, as with the J21s, their numbers were considerably reduced between 1948 and 1949. The last survivors of the class were not finally withdrawn until 1962; despite this late date, none have survived.

Examples of the J25 class were to be seen at York depot in the fifties, with six being allocated at this time. No. 65685 was an example of the original saturated design with slide valves, built in 1899 and withdrawn in September 1959

23.9.56

Awaiting its next duty at Hull Botanic Gardens shed was no. 65655 built in 1898. This engine was withdrawn in December 1958. As with the J21s the J25 class was fitted with a large spacious cab

23.9.56

J25 no. 65717, seen here at Tyne Dock, was an example of this class rebuilt with superheater and piston valves. Note the extended smokebox. J25s were in action as bankers at Tyne Dock until the early sixties. No. 65717 was withdrawn in October 1958

7.7.56

J26 class 0–6–0 4F

Designer: W. Worsdell. Introduced for the North Eastern Railway in 1904.
Total built: 50, built at Gateshead and Darlington works, 1904–5. All survived to be taken over by British Railways and were allocated number series 65730–79.

Principal dimensions

Weight:	Locomotive	46 tons 16 cwt
	Tender	36 tons 19 cwt
Boiler pressure:		180 lb/sq in
Driving wheels:		4 ft 7¼ in
Tractive effort:		24,640 lb
Cylinders:		(2) 18½ x 26 in

Stephenson motion.

The class remained intact until four were withdrawn in June 1958. Engines were then condemned steadily until they finally became extinct in 1962.

Thirty-five of the J26 class were allocated to Newport depot during the mid-fifties, including no. 65740, seen here at its home shed. Built at Darlington in 1904 this engine remained in service until January 1959

8.7.56

J27 class 0–6–0 4F

Designer: T.W. Worsdell, developed from the earlier J26 class. The J27s made their appearance on the North Eastern Railway in 1906.
Total built: 115. Darlington works built the majority, a total of sixty-five locomotives. Three private companies were also involved, North British Locomotive Co. building twenty, Beyer, Peacock & Co. also twenty, and the remaining ten built by Robert Stephenson & Co. Construction was between 1906 and 1923, all transferring into BR stock, number series 65780–894.

Principal dimensions

Weight:	Locomotive	47 tons
	Tender	36 tons 19 cwt
Boiler pressure:		180 lb/sq in
Driving wheels:		4 ft 7¼ in
Tractive effort:		24,640 lb
Cylinders:		(2) 18½ in x 26 in

Stephenson motion.

These powerful and popular 0–6–0s were to be found throughout the North Eastern region employed on a wide range of duties. The J27s were to remain intact until 1959 when twenty-one were withdrawn, examples of the class remaining in service almost to the end of steam.

One still remains, no. 65894, which was purchased for preservation and has become a well-known engine on the North Yorkshire Moors Railway, restored with its former LNER no. 2392. This particular engine was the last example built, being completed in September 1923.

J27 no. 65881 was built in 1922 at Darlington. This is an example of the superheated engines. When the picture was taken this J27 was still in superheated form; this was later removed in 1961. Note the extended smokebox

Selby depot, 23.9.56

This picture of no. 65827, built in 1908 by the North British Locomotive Co., shows the class in its original condition, the last batch being built as superheated engines. No. 65827, seen here at Malton, remained in service until July 1959

23.9.56

Fresh from general overhaul, no. 65805 was photographed at Haverton Hill depot. It was built in 1908 at Darlington works, withdrawal from service being in January 1966

8.7.56

J38 class 0–6–0 6F

Designer: H.N. Gresley. Introduced in 1926 for the LNER.
Total built: 35 at Darlington works, being completed between January and May inclusive of that year. All were taken into British Railways stock, receiving nos. 65900–34.

Principal dimensions

Weight:	Locomotive	58 tons 19 cwt
	Tender	44 tons 4 cwt
Boiler pressure:		180 lb/sq in
Driving wheels:		4 ft 8 in
Tractive effort:		28,415 lb
Cylinders:		(2) 20 in x 26 in

Stephenson valve gear – piston valves.

The J38s were all to be found in the Scottish region where their principal duties were coal traffic. The class remained intact until 1962 when two, nos. 65923 and 65928, were withdrawn in December. Withdrawals proceeded steadily until the last two, nos. 65901 and 65929, were withdrawn in April 1967. They in fact were the last two Gresley-designed engines to remain in service with British Railways. None have survived into preservation.

The J38s could easily be mistaken for the J39 class which appeared in 1926. Among the major differences were smaller driving wheels, a longer boiler and a shorter smokebox. This class was to be found at the Scottish region depots, the last survivors remaining until 1967. No. 65922, pictured here at St Margaret's, remained in service until October 1966

21.8.55

F4 class 2–4–2T 1P

Designer: T.W. Worsdell for the Great Eastern Railway.
Total built: 118, 1884–1909.

Principal dimensions

Weight:	53 tons 19 cwt
Boiler pressure:	160 lb/sq in
Driving wheels:	5 ft 8 in
Tractive effort:	14,170 lb
Cylinders:	(2) 17½ in x 24 in

Stephenson motion – slide valves.

In 1955 only two locomotives remained in service, no. 67157 and no. 67162, which was withdrawn in the August. No. 67157 was not withdrawn until June 1956. In later years this engine had worked on the St Combs branch in the north of Scotland, eventually being replaced by LMS design class 2MT 2–6–0s. In its final months it was employed as a works shunter at Inverurie works.

Still intact at Stratford works and awaiting scrapping was F4 no. 67174 of Lowestoft depot, from where it was withdrawn in December 1954. Note the Westinghouse pump and the stovepipe chimney which many of the class carried. In the distance is one of the last J70 'Tram' engines to be withdrawn, no. 68225, condemned in March 1955

7.5.55

This F4 no. 67157 was sent to the north of Scotland in 1948 and allocated to Aberdeen Kittybrewster depot, where this picture was taken. The F4 was used on the St Combs branch until replaced by more modern motive power. This working was the reason that 'cowcatchers' were fitted to the locomotive

24.8.55

F5 class 2–4–2T 2P

Designer: S.D. Holden for the Great Eastern Railway in 1911.
These engines were rebuilt from the earlier F4 class. Numbered 67188–67219.

Principal dimensions

Weight:	53 tons 19 cwt
Boiler pressure:	180 lb/sq in
Driving wheels:	5 ft 4 in
Tractive effort:	15,750 lb
Cylinders:	(2) 17½ in x 24 in

Stephenson motion.

Many of the duties which were performed by the ex-GER 2–4–2Ts had been taken over by other locomotives by the mid-fifties. At a number of depots F5s and F6s were to be seen in store. In 1955 withdrawals of the F5s commenced; within three short years all had been condemned.

Despite the outward appearance of F5 no. 67192 at Stratford in 1955, this locomotive was to remain in service for another three years until withdrawn in May 1958, making it one of the last survivors of its class. Twenty F5s were allocated to Stratford depot early in 1955

7.5.55

Another of the Stratford F5s was no. 67215, seen here fitted with a stovepipe chimney. Time was running out for this locomotive as it was withdrawn four months after this photograph was taken, on a particularly grey, dismal day

7.5.55

F6 class 2–4–2T 2P

Designer: S.D. Holden, locomotive superintendent of the Great Eastern Railway 1908–12. This design was the final development of the 2–4–2Ts. The F6s made their appearance in 1911.

Total built: 20. The F6s were allocated BR nos. 67220–39. The engines remained intact until 1955 when they, like the F5s, were all withdrawn during the following three years.

Principal dimensions

Weight:	56 tons 9 cwt
Boiler pressure:	180 lb/sq in
Driving wheels:	5 ft 4 in
Tractive effort:	17,570 lb
Cylinders:	(2) 17½ in x 24 in

Cambridge depot had no. 67238 in its allocation for a number of years together with other class members on occasions. During 1955 this engine was to be seen stored at the back of the locomotive depot, usually accompanied by several E4 2–4–0s, one of which was no. 62785, the sole survivor. Unfortunately no examples of the Great Eastern 2–4–2Ts were so lucky.

During the early fifties F6 class 2–4–2Ts were usually to be seen at Cambridge, nos. 67227/38 being allocated to the depot. This picture of no. 67227 was taken during a break from its usual carriage pilot duties. The engine remained in service until May 1958

10.4.53

G5 class 0–4–4T 2P

Designer: T.W. Worsdell. Introduced to the North Eastern Railway in 1894.
Total built: 110. Constructed at Darlington works, 1894–1901. Numbered 67240–67349.

Principal dimensions

Weight:	Locomotive	54 tons 4 cwt
Boiler pressure:		160 lb/sq in
Driving wheels:		5 ft 1¼ in
Tractive effort:		17,265 lb
Cylinders:		(2) 18 in x 24 in

Stephenson motion – slide valves.

Several locomotives were fitted for push-pull working, some having been rebuilt with larger tanks. All were still in service when taken over by British Railways. Withdrawals commenced within months of the take-over; by 1958 all had been condemned, the last ten in service in the December.

During the fifties four G5s could be found allocated to Cambridge depot, their principal duties being the Audley End–Bartlow branch. Other members of the class were widely distributed, mainly in the North Eastern region.

This G5 is an example of the class fitted for push-pull work, photographed at Hull Botanic Gardens depot. This locomotive was built at Darlington works in 1895 and remained in service until October 1958. Note the Hopper-type bunker fitted

23.9.56

This G5 was at Doncaster shed making its final journey to Darlington works. No. 67269 was one of the G5s allocated to Cambridge where they were used on the Audley End–Bartlow service. The locomotive was push-pull, fitted with compressed-air type equipment. Many of the G5s were withdrawn about this time

23.9.56

C12 class 4–4–2T 2P

Designer: H.A. Ivatt for the Great Northern Railway. Introduced in 1898.
Total built: 60, Doncaster works, 1898–1907. Forty-nine of these were handed over to British Railways, although six did not last long, being withdrawn during that same year. Thereafter withdrawals took place steadily until the class became extinct in 1958. Numbered 67350–67398.

Principal dimensions

Weight:	62 tons 6 cwt
Boiler pressure:	170 lb/sq in
Driving wheels:	5 ft 8 in
Tractive effort:	17,900 lb
Cylinders:	(2) 18 in x 26 in

Stephenson gear – slide valves.

During the early fifties New England depot had a sizeable number of these sturdy tank locomotives which were used as carriage pilots, local branch workings and station pilots. Among their duties was banking heavy northbound expresses out of Peterborough station, which had quite a severe curve. The C12s blasted through the station, their sharp exhaust echoing back from the overall station roof which existed at that time.

Cambridge depot had no. 67360 in its allocation for several years. Here the engine stands ready to depart from the south-end bay platform. Not long after this picture was taken the C12 joined the 'stored' row at the back of the depot. The engine was finally withdrawn in January 1955

10.4.53

Members of the C12 class were often stored for short periods at New England. No. 67366 was in company with a J52 when photographed. It was returned to traffic and withdrawn in April 1958. Note the tarpaulin sheeting over the chimney; this was commonplace at the time when engines were placed in store. These were well greased and often coaled up to be returned to traffic if necessary in the minimum amount of time

13.3.55

C13 class 4–4–2T 2P

Designer: J.G. Robinson. His first tank design for suburban work. Introduced on the Great Central Railway in 1903.
Total built: 40. Vulcan Foundry and Gorton works, 1903–5.

Principal dimensions

Weight:	66 tons 13 cwt
Boiler pressure:	160 lb/sq in
Driving wheels:	5 ft 7 in
Tractive effort:	17,100 lb
Cylinders:	(2) 18 in x 26 in

Stephenson motion – slide valves.

The entire class passed into British Railways' ownership receiving the number series 67400–39. Five years later withdrawals commenced. One engine (no. 67417) survived for two years longer than the remainder of the class and was withdrawn in January 1960. Several locomotives were fitted for push-pull working. The C14 class of twelve locomotives was very similar (67440–67451), having increased tank and bunker capacity.

Three members of the C13 class were still to be found at Neasdon depot in the mid-fifties, all of which were fitted for push-pull working. No. 67420 was standing in the depot yard with a WD 2–8–0 and N5 0–6–2T for company

20.3.55

C15 class 4–4–2T 2P

Designer: W.P. Reid, locomotive superintendent. Introduced in 1911 for the North British Railway.
Total built: 30. The Yorkshire Engine Co., 1911–13. All survived to become BR nos. 67452–81.

Principal dimensions

Weight:	68 tons 15 cwt
Boiler pressure:	175 lb/sq in
Driving wheels:	5 ft 9 in
Tractive effort:	18,160 lb
Cylinders:	(2) 18 in x 26 in

Stephenson motion – slide valves.

During the fifties the class found little work: their duties were often station pilots, shunting and so on. There were exceptions among these, those which were fitted for push-pull working, two of which ended their days on the Craigendoran–Arrochar service. These considerably outlived their classmates, not being withdrawn until April 1960. The others were all withdrawn between 1953 and 1956. As with the C16 4–4–2Ts, none survive.

Two C15 4–4–2Ts were allocated to Thornton depot, one of which was no. 67452, photographed at its home depot. This was the first member of the class to enter service, being completed by the Yorkshire Engine Co. in December 1911. It was withdrawn in February 1956

23.8.55

Time had nearly run out for C15 no. 67463 at Polmont when I took this picture of her on a grey summer's day. The following month the locomotive was withdrawn. During the mid-fifties Polmont had four C15s and a solitary C16 in its allocation

22.8.55

C16 class 4–4–2T 2P

These engines were very similar in appearance to the earlier C15s. Two important differences being they were superheated and had piston valves.

Designer: W.P. Reid. Introduced in 1915.

Total built: 21. The North British Locomotive Co., 1915–21. The entire class became BR nos. 67482–502.

Principal dimensions

Weight:	72 tons 10 cwt
Boiler pressure:	165 lb/sq in
Driving wheels:	5 ft 9 in
Tractive effort:	19,080 lb
Cylinders:	(2) 19 in x 26 in

Stephenson motion – piston valves.

During the fifties C16s could be found at a number of Scottish region depots, their duties including passenger and stock workings. Withdrawals commenced in 1955 with two of the class. The last survivor was no. 67485, which was withdrawn in April 1961.

By the mid-fifties many of the C16s found little work. No. 67486 was lying idle, temporarily stored, when this picture was taken of it in Dundee shed. No. 67486 remained in service for almost a further five years, being withdrawn in April 1960

23.8.55

V1 and V3 class 2–6–2T 4MT

Designer: H.N. Gresley for the LNER. V1 class introduced in 1930. V3 class developed from V1 class introduced in 1939. Nos. 67682 onwards were built as V3 class, others were rebuilt from V1 design.
Total built: V1 82, V3 10. Rebuilding of the V1 class commenced in 1940 and was to continue until 1961. Numbered 67600–91.

Principal dimensions

	V1 class	V3 class
Weight:	84 tons	86 tons 16 cwt
Boiler pressure:	180 lb/sq in	200 lb/sq in
Driving wheels:	5 ft 8 in	5 ft 8 in
Tractive effort:	22,465 lb	24,960 lb
Cylinders:	(3) 16 in x 26 in	16 in x 26 in

Walschaerts valve gear and derived motion – 8 in piston valves.

These very useful locomotives were mainly employed on local passenger and suburban trains. Occasionally they were to be seen on short freight-trip workings and parcel traffic, especially in their later days, when many of the duties which they previously worked had been taken over by diesel railcars.

During the fifties they were all to be found in the North-East and Scotland, with the majority being south of the border.

Both classes remained intact until 1960 when one from each of the V1 and V3 classes was withdrawn; the remaining V1 class locomotives were withdrawn at the end of 1962, leaving just twenty-six V3s in service. This number was halved the following year, with the final thirteen being withdrawn in 1963. Unfortunately no examples of either class have survived into preservation.

Another view of V1 no. 67647, this showing the Hopper-type bunker fitted to the locomotive. Many of the later-built V1s and the V3s were fitted with these

Heaton, 8.7.56

This particular V1 class locomotive no. 67602 was one of the original batch built in 1930 at Doncaster works. It was never rebuilt to V3, being withdrawn in May 1962

Eastfield depot, 26.8.55

V3 no. 67646 awaiting its turn for coaling at Heaton depot. This locomotive was fitted with the plain bunker. Twelve V class tanks were allocated to this depot during the mid-fifties

8.7.56

Shining like a new pin, V1 class no. 67618 had just been through Darlington works for a general overhaul. This locomotive was on Scottish region stock, allocated to 65E Kipps. Rebuilding to V3 in this case was in 1958, the engine remaining in service until December 1962

8.7.56

This locomotive, no. 67687, was one of the original V3 class built in December 1939. The engine had just received a general overhaul at Darlington works and was being watered ready to return to its home depot

Blaydon, 7.7.56

L1 class 2–6–4T 4MT

Designer: E. Thompson. Introduced in 1945 for the LNER.
Total built: 100. The first was built in 1945 at Doncaster. No more appeared until nationalization when twenty-nine were completed at Darlington works. Two further batches of thirty-five each completed the total, one batch from the North British Locomotive Co., 1948–9 and the final thirty-five from Robert Stephenson and Hawthorns, 1949–50. Numbered 67701–67800.

Principal dimensions

Weight:	89 tons 9 cwt
Boiler pressure:	225 lb/sq in
Driving wheels:	5 ft 2 in
Tractive effort:	32,080 lb
Cylinders:	(2) 20 in x 26 in

Walschaerts valve gear – piston valves.

L1s were employed on many passenger duties, empty stock workings and even freight workings. They were widely distributed and were to be found in both the Eastern and North Eastern regions in the mid-fifties. Around this time they were to be frequently seen on King's Cross–Peterborough local passenger workings. As with 2–6–4Ts of other designs throughout the country, the ever-increasing tide of diesel multiple units coming into service took over many of their duties. Withdrawals were in a comparatively short period of time: 1960–2. No example has survived into preservation.

No. 67790 was employed on a short pick-up goods on the East Coast main line when photographed at Huntingdon. The L1s were fitted with electric lighting, although a handlamp can be seen in use above the light on the far side of the buffer beams

15.4.55

The cabs on the L1s received modification during service, as initially complaints were received about them being draughty. No. 67741 was one of the batch of thirty-five built by the North British Locomotive Co. in 1948; it was among the last withdrawn in December 1962

10.8.54

J94 class 0–6–0ST 4F

Designer: R.A. Riddles. An 'Austerity' design introduced in 1943 for the Ministry of Supply.

Principal dimensions

Weight:	48 tons 5 cwt
Boiler pressure:	170 lb/sq in
Driving wheels:	4 ft 3 in
Tractive effort:	23,870 lb
Cylinders:	(2) 18 in x 26 in

Stephenson valve gear – slide valves.

The 'Austerity' designs were capable of operating on the British railway system as well as on the Continent. Three types made their appearance in 1943, the 2–8–0, 2–10–0 and 0–6–0ST, the later based on the standard Hunslet 18 in design with modifications. Construction was carried out by several companies and was to run for several years.

In 1946 the LNER agreed to purchase seventy-five of these locomotives, which became class J94. These included engines built by six different companies:

R. Stephenson and Hawthorns	7
Hudswell, Clarke & Co.	14
Hunslet Engine Co.	14
Vulcan Foundry	14
W.G. Bagnall & Co.	16
Andrew Barclay & Co.	10

These engines were numbered 8006–080, later to become BR nos. 68006–80. They were used at several locations, with a considerable number in the North East. The J94 was also found to be very suitable for the Cromford and High Peak line where they took over from the ageing North London 0–6–0Ts. At other locations the J94s were principally used on shunting and short-trip workings.

The J94s remained intact until 1960 when six were withdrawn. Several members of the class were sold to the National Coal Board and other users. Two of these, nos. 68077 and 68078, have survived into preservation, both built by Andrew Barclay. The last member of the class in BR service was no. 68012 which was withdrawn in October 1967.

Several other examples of this design exist at various preservation sites carrying numbers similar to the BR series. These were not locomotives purchased by the LNER from the Ministry of Supply.

No. 68037 busily engaged in shunting operations at Darlington. These sturdily built locomotives were employed on this work, and occasional short-trip workings. No. 68037 was built by the Vulcan Foundry in July 1945 and allocated WD no. 75322. It remained in service until May 1965

7.7.56

This example of the J94 class no. 68060 was one of the batch built by Hudswell, Clarke & Co., in this case being completed in September 1945. The engine number is carried on the tank sides, typical of Darlington works practice

Darlington, 2.5.64

Y7 and Y8 class 0–4–0T 0F

These two classes were very similar in appearance.
Designer: T.W. Worsdell for the North Eastern Railway. Y7 introduced 1888, Y8 introduced 1890.

Principal dimensions

	Y7	Y8
Weight:	22 tons 14 cwt	15 tons 10 cwt
Boiler pressure:	140 lb/sq in	140 lb/sq in
Driving wheels:	3 ft 6½ in	3 ft 0 in
Tractive effort:	11,040 lb	6,000 lb
Cylinders:	(2) 14 in x 20 in	11 in x 15 in

No Y7 class locomotives remained in BR service in 1955. However, two did exist in private ownership, both of which have survived into preservation so are included in this title. The two engines concerned were both in use at collieries. BR no. 68088 was withdrawn in 1948 and transferred to departmental stock until 1952 when purchased by the National Coal Board. The engine is currently at the Great Central Railway. The other Y7 was sold in LNER days and is now at the Middleton Railway.

Two class Y8s were taken into British Railways stock, one was withdrawn in 1948. The sole survivor, no. 68091, was employed as shed pilot at York. In 1954 it was renumbered departmental no. 55 and withdrawn in November 1956. Unfortunately it has not survived into preservation.

This picture shows Y7 no. 68088 in preservation at the Great Central Railway, Loughborough. Both the surviving Y7s were sold to private owners and rescued from them for preservation. This engine was rescued from the National Coal Board

22.2.92

Y9 class 0–4–0 0F

Designer: M. Holmes. Introduced in 1882 for the North British Railway.
Total built: 38. Most were built between 1882 and 1899 at Cowlairs works; the first two pioneer engines were both built by Neilson & Co. in 1882. Thirty-three remained in service to be taken over by British Railways, numbered 68092–124.

Principal dimensions

Weight:	Locomotive	27 tons 16 cwt
	Tender (where permanently fitted)	6 tons
Boiler pressure:		130 lb/sq in
Driving wheels		3 ft 8 in
Tractive effort:		9,845 lb
Cylinders:		(2) 14 in x 20 in

Stephenson valve gear – slide valves.

Several of the class ran with wooden tenders of various shapes and sizes to supplement the very small amount of coal carried on the locomotive. The Y9s were fitted with wooden buffer beams and buffers.

St Margaret's depot had a number of Y9s in its allocation: several of these were sub-shedded to South Leith and Seafield, being employed on shunting duties at Leith Docks and elsewhere.

Other members of the class were to be found at various Scottish depots. These engines were commonly referred to by enginemen as 'Pugs'.

Withdrawals took place steadily throughout the fifties; only eight remained at the start of the next decade. The last to remain in stock was no. 68095 which was withdrawn in December 1962. Built in 1887 this Y9 completed seventy-five years service. Fortunately this very interesting engine has survived into preservation and is now to be found at the Bo'ness and Kinneil Railway.

The coal capacity of the Y9 class was a maximum of 18 cwt. This resulted in many members running with four-wheeled wooden coal tenders. When these were in use no coal was carried on the engine itself, although the tenders were difficult to work from.

No. 68123 was one of the Y9s which worked without a tender. Here the engine is seen in Dundee depot; note the spark arrestor. Y9s, known by enginemen as 'Pugs', were used on many tightly curved factory sidings, docks and so on

23.8.55

This picture shows one of the wooden tenders fitted to the Y9s, which ranged considerably in size and shape. No. 68104 was pictured at South Leith sub-shed. Built in 1890 this Y9 was among the last in service, being withdrawn in October 1962 after completing a remarkable seventy-two years in service

21.8.55

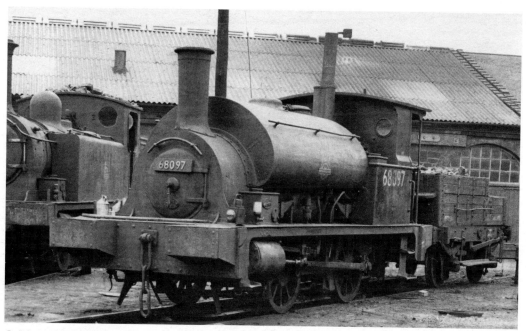

St Margaret's depot open-tank engine roundhouse would usually have had several of the depot's Y9s on shed during the early fifties. No. 68097 was one of the batch built at Cowlairs works in 1887. As with many of the St Margaret's engines it ran with a permanently attached wooden tender. This particular Y9 remained in service until October 1958

21.8.55

Y4 class 0–4–0T 0F

Designer: A.J. Hill. Introduced in 1913 for the Great Eastern Railway.
Total built: 5. The first locomotive was completed in November 1913, two more followed in 1914 and a further two in 1921, one of which was in departmental stock for most of its life. Numbered 68125–68129.

Principal dimensions

Weight:	38 tons 1 cwt
Boiler pressure:	180 lb/sq in
Driving wheels:	3 ft 10 in
Tractive effort:	19,225 lb
Cylinders:	(2) 17 in x 20 in

Walschaerts valve gear – slide valves.

These powerful, sturdy side tanks were built at Stratford works, principally for shunting duties on the goods yards and sidings in East London. These abounded with tight curves, hence the requirement for short-wheelbase tank locomotives. As will be seen from the picture below, dumb buffers were fitted to prevent buffer locking.

The duties of the Y4s (apart from the departmental engine) were taken over by diesels in the mid-fifties. The first to be withdrawn was no. 68125 in September 1955, followed by two in 1956 and another in 1957. The departmental engine continued in use at Stratford works until 1963, being condemned in December of that year. No examples have survived.

No. 68125 was the first of the five Y4s to be withdrawn, just four months after this photograph of the engine was taken at Stratford. Note the dumb buffers and coal supply in front of the cab. The engine was in a very grimy state, which makes it almost impossible to see the small numbers on the tank side

7.5.55

Y1 and Y3 class 0–4–0T

Designer: Sentinel Company.

Designed and built by the Sentinel Company, the single-speed geared Y1 class was introduced in 1925 and the two-speed geared Y3s in 1927.

Both classes operated at 275 lb/sq in boiler pressure, with cylinders 6¾ in x 9 in, rotary cam and poppet valves and 2 ft 6 in driving wheels. Numbered 68130–68185 (Y1 and Y3).

Many examples of both classes were to be found in departmental service during the fifties. Inroads were made into the engines in running stock during the mid-fifties; others were transferred to departmental stock at this time, with the last two examples of these Y3 departmental nos. 7 and 40 being condemned in May 1964.

One example of the Y1 class has survived; this was no. 68153, later to become departmental no. 54, which on withdrawal in June 1961 was purchased by the Middleton Railway.

The sole surviving ex-LNER Sentinel is Y1 class no. 54. Works no. 8837 of 1933 this locomotive was allocated no. 68153, becoming departmental no. 54 in October 1954. The engine was withdrawn in June 1961 and purchased by the Middleton Railway. This photograph shows the engine working on the North Yorkshire Moors Railway at Grosmont

15.5.91

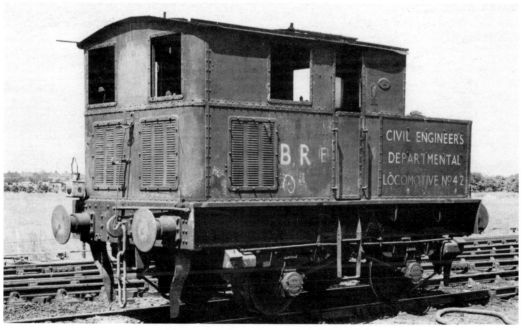

This Y3 class locomotive was transferred to departmental stock in September 1942. In March 1953 it became no. 42. Built by Sentinels as works no. 8331 in 1930 it spent its later years at Chesterton Permanent Way depot where this photograph was taken, being condemned in July 1960

23.6.57

Z4 and Z5 class 0–4–2T 0F

These two classes were built by Manning Wardle & Co. for the Great North of Scotland Railway. Both were introduced in 1915.
Designer: Manning Wardle & Co.
Total built: Z4 – 2 (nos. 68190–1). Z5 – 2 (nos. 68192–3).

Principal dimensions

	Z4	Z5
Weight:	25 tons 17 cwt	30 tons 18 cwt
Boiler pressure:	160 lb/sq in	160 lb/sq in
Driving wheels:	3 ft 6 in	4 ft 0 in
Tractive effort:	10,945 lb	11,105 lb
Cylinders:	(2) 13 in x 20 in	14 in x 20 in

Both had Stephenson valve gear – slide valves.

These 0–4–2Ts were principally employed on shunting work at Aberdeen Docks (depending on traffic two were usually in steam) in the mid-fifties. The others were at Aberdeen Kittybrewster shed, as was the case in August 1955 when the photos below were taken. The first to be withdrawn was Z5 no. 68193 in April 1956 followed by Z4 no. 68191 in March 1959. The remaining two engines, Z4 no. 68190 and Z5 no. 68192, were both withdrawn in April 1960. None survive.

Z4 class no. 68191, busily shunting on a grey misty morning at Aberdeen Docks. This was the first Z4 to be withdrawn in March 1959. These unusual engines, built by Manning Wardle & Co. of Leeds, were a familiar sight on the docks from their inception way back in 1915

24.8.55

No. 68193 one of the two Z5 class; in this case it was still lettered British Railways. When photographed it was lying out of use at the back of Aberdeen Kittybrewster depot. No. 68193 was the first Z5 withdrawn in April 1956

24.8.55

J71 class 0–6–0T 0F

Designer: T.W. Worsdell. Introduced by the North Eastern Railway in 1886.
Total built: 120. All were built at Darlington works between 1886 and 1895; eighty came into BR stock. Withdrawals commenced in the 1930s. The last survivor was withdrawn in February 1961. Numbered 68230–68316.

Principal dimensions

Weight:	37 tons 12 cwt
Boiler pressure:	140 lb/sq in
Driving wheels:	4 ft 7¼ in

Locomotives in this class had several cylinder sizes and of course different tractive efforts. The majority of J71s in service had 16 in x 22 in cylinders and a tractive effort of 12,130 lb.

During the fifties J71s were to be found at widely scattered depots, all of which were part of the North Eastern region.

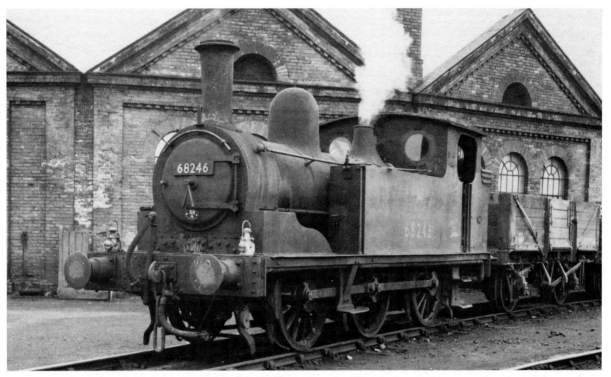

No. 68246, fitted with steam and vacuum ejector, standing in the open York South depot. This example was completed at Darlington in July 1889, remaining in service until November 1958

23.9.56

No. 68230 was the oldest example of the J71s to come into BR service. Completed in November 1886 it remained in stock until January 1960, completing seventy-four years. This picture of no. 68230 was taken at Hull Botanic Gardens depot where the engine was on the ash-pit duty. The engine was fitted with steam brake only

23.9.56

J88 class 0–6–0T 0F

These engines were introduced by the North British Railway in 1908 principally for dock shunting duties, the locomotives having a short wheelbase.
Designer: W.P. Reid, locomotive superintendent NBR, 1903–19.
Total built: 35. British Railways took over all members of the class, which had been built at Cowlairs works between 1904 and 1919. The number series allocated was 68320–54.

Principal dimensions

Weight:	38 tons 14 cwt
Boiler pressure:	130 lb/sq in
Driving wheels:	3 ft 9 in
Tractive effort:	12,155 lb
Cylinders:	(2 outside) 15 in x 22 in

Stephenson motion – slide valves.

Many of the J88s were still engaged on dock shunting during the fifties. Several could be found at Leith docks and also working from several other Scottish depots.

The first to go was no. 68341, after falling into a harbour. This was the start of steady withdrawals. The last survivor was no. 68345 which was condemned in December 1962, thus rendering a very distinctive NBR class extinct.

This J88 was one of the last to remain in service, being withdrawn in October 1962. When photographed it was trundling back to its depot, Thornton. Note the very distinctive tall chimney and short wheelbase, as well as the solid buffers. No. 68335 was one of two to be fitted with vacuum ejectors; the remainder all had steam brakes

23.8.55

Most of the J88s had steam brakes only. No. 68345 was the last survivor of the class, being withdrawn in December 1962. The engine is seen here at Dunfermline depot. Note the base of a spark arrestor fitting on the chimney

23.8.55

J73 class 0–6–0T 3F

Designer: T.W. Worsdell. Introduced in 1891 for the North Eastern Railway.
Total built: 10, 1891–2. All of these survived to be taken over by British Railways, receiving the numbers 68355–64.

Principal dimensions

Weight:	46 tons 15 cwt
Boiler pressure:	160 lb/sq in
Driving wheels:	4 ft 7¼ in
Tractive effort:	21,320 lb
Cylinders:	(2) 19 in x 24 in

Joy gear – slide valves.

All members of this powerful class were built at Gateshead works; during the fifties they were to be found in the North Eastern region. The first to be withdrawn was no. 68358 in May 1955, with another in 1957, three in 1958 and two in 1960. The last three survivors went in 1960, no. 68361, being the last in service, was condemned in November.

Hull Alexandra Dock, where this picture was taken, was a sub-shed of Springhead depot. The J73 class locomotives were employed on short-trip workings. No. 68360 was among the last to remain in service until February 1960, ending its days on the scrap road at Darlington works the following month

23.9.56

J77 class 0–6–0T 2F

Designer: T.W. Worsdell. Introduced in 1899 for the North Eastern Railway, rebuilding taking place from 1899 to 1921. Numbered 68391–68440.
Total built: 60. These engines were all rebuilds of Fletcher 0–4–4Ts built between 1874 and 1884.

Principal dimensions

Weight:	43 tons
Boiler pressure:	160 lb/sq in
Driving wheels:	4 ft 1¼ in
Tractive effort:	17,560 lb
Cylinders:	(2) 17 in x 22 in

Stephenson valve gear – slide valves.

The J77s were rebuilt at Darlington and York, the latter being easily distinguished by their rounded cabs. The twenty Darlington rebuilds have a square-cornered cab roof.

This was by and large a very long-lived class, the last example remaining in service until 1961, although withdrawals had commenced as early as 1933. Forty-six J77s were taken over by BR, with a small number of these being withdrawn shortly afterwards.

During the fifties the entire class was to be found in the North Eastern region at widely scattered locations. Two further locomotives which had been sold to the Ministry of Fuel and Power were still at work, one being withdrawn in the mid-fifties, the other remaining in service until the early sixties. Unfortunately, not one example has survived into preservation.

No. 68399 was originally built as an 0–4–4T in 1875 by Hawthorn & Co., being rebuilt to J77 class at York in 1902. Remaining in service until April 1958, in the following month it was cut up at Darlington works

North Blyth depot, 7.7.56

J83 class 0–6–0T 2F

Designer: M. Holmes for the North British Railway. Introduced in 1900, all were built by private companies.
Total built: 40, 1900–1, twenty each by Neilson, Reid & Co. and Sharp, Stewart Co. One was withdrawn in 1947; all the others were handed over to British Railways and allocated number series 68442–81.

Principal dimensions

Weight:	45 tons 5 cwt
Boiler pressure:	150 lb/sq in
Driving wheels:	4 ft 6 in
Tractive effort:	17,745 lb
Cylinders:	(2) 17 in x 26 in
Stephenson motion.	

The class was quite widespread in BR days. St Margaret's and Haymarket depots, Edinburgh, especially the former, had a sizeable allocation. They were also to be found at Eastfield, Thornton and many other depots. Withdrawals commenced in the mid-fifties, with the final engines lasting until 1962. None survive.

No. 68465 on typical shunting duties at Dundee. This was one of the engines built by Sharp, Stewart Co. in 1901. It was among the first class members withdrawn, in this case in August 1957

23.8.55

Two of Thornton depot's J83s, nos. 68451 and 68453, await their next duty. Both were built by Neilson, Reid & Co. in 1900 and 1901 respectively. No. 68451 was withdrawn in February 1953; no. 68453 remained in service until October 1962 and was among the last survivors of the class

23.8.55

J67 and J69 class 0–6–0T 2F

Designer: J. Holden for the Great Eastern Railway.
Total built: 160 at Stratford works from 1890 to 1904. The main external difference between these two classes was the larger tanks fitted to the J69s.

Principal dimensions

Weight:	40 tons (with slight variations)
Boiler pressure:	(J67) 160 lb/sq in
	(J69) 180 lb/sq in
Driving wheels:	4 ft 0 in
Tractive effort:	(J67) 16,970 lb
	(J69) 19,090 lb
Cylinders:	(2) 16½ in x 22 in

Stephenson motion.

These locomotives were numbered within the series 68490–636. There were several variations, the most numerous were the J69/1s which were introduced in 1902, with larger tanks and fireboxes; some were rebuilds of the J67 class, others a new construction. British Railways took over 134 locomotives of J67 and J69 classes, which consisted of shunting and passenger engines. The last withdrawals were in September 1962.

Locomotives of these classes were widely distributed in the fifties, in areas such as Scotland, Liverpool, Manchester and Hitchin together with many East Anglian depots.

One locomotive has been preserved, J69 no. 68633, built at Stratford in 1904 and withdrawn in November 1960. It is now at the National Railway Museum, York.

No. 68496 was on loan to the Peterborough Sugar Beet factory when photographed. This engine, built in 1890, was an example of the J67 class, remaining in service until May 1956

4.12.54

This engine, no. 68550, is a J69/1 seen here at Stratford. Many of these locomotives were in service with stovepipe chimneys. This J69 class was a development of the J67 with large tanks and fireboxes. No. 68550 was built at Stratford in 1904 being withdrawn in July 1961

7.5.55

This J69/1 is an example of the class fitted with a vacuum ejector, photographed at Lincoln depot. Built originally as a J67 in 1900, this engine was rebuilt to J69/1 specifications in 1916. These engines were to be found at many depots even as far away from their original GER territory as Scotland

25.9.57

J68 class 0–6–0T 3F

These sturdy tank locomotives were a development of the J69 class with side-window cabs.
Designer: A.J. Hill.
Total built: 30 at Stratford works, twenty between 1912 and 1914, the final batch of ten in 1923. All except one were handed over to British Railways and numbered 68638–66.

Principal dimensions

Weight:	42 tons 9 cwt
Boiler pressure:	180 lb/sq in
Driving wheels:	4 ft 0 in
Tractive effort:	19,090 lb
Cylinders:	(2) 16½ in x 22 in

Stephenson motion – slide valves.

The entire class was withdrawn between 1958 and 1961. Only three, nos. 68642, 68646 and 68649, remained in service to be withdrawn in the September of 1961. None survive.

This locomotive was the second of the class to be constructed in 1912. No. 68638 was photographed at Hitchin depot in rather a shabby state – note the rust on the chimney. The Westinghouse pump was badly dented, possibly due to frequent blows with a coal hammer, a not infrequent occurrence! No. 68638 remained in service until February 1959

14.10.56

J72 class 0–6–0T 2F

Designer: T.W. Worsdell. Introduced in 1898 for the North Eastern Railway.
Total built: 113 by Darlington and Doncaster works and Armstrong Whitworth & Co. Numbered 68670–68754, 69001–69028.

Principal dimensions

Weight:	38 tons 12 cwt
Boiler pressure:	140 lb/sq in
Driving wheels:	4 ft 1¼ in
Tractive effort:	16,760 lb
Cylinders:	(2) 17 in x 24 in

Stephenson valve gear – slide valves.

Although the first J72 was completed at Darlington works in December 1898, it was not until May 1951 that the last member of the class was turned out, also from Darlington. Twenty-eight locomotives of this very useful class were in fact built by British Railways from 1949 to 1951, receiving the numbers 69001–28.

The J72 was very similar in appearance to the earlier J71s, the principal difference being larger cylinders and smaller wheels. The first twenty of the British Railways-built engines were completed with steam brake only, with five receiving vacuum ejectors from 1937 onwards. The final eight built in 1951 were constructed with steam brake, vacuum ejectors and carriage heating equipment.

The majority of the class were to be found in the North Eastern region during the fifties. Exceptions were to be found in Scotland, some working on the old Great North of Scotland territory.

Delivery of diesel shunters in ever increasing numbers was soon to make its presence felt, the first J72 being withdrawn in 1958. Withdrawals took place in ever increasing numbers until 1964, when the last in general service was withdrawn. Two were transferred to departmental stock, receiving nos. 58 and 59 at the time. Fortunately, one of these locomotives has survived into preservation, no. 69023 being purchased on withdrawal in September 1966.

Two J72s received special treatment in 1960, when both were repainted in the North Eastern green livery following overhaul. These two locomotives, nos. 68723 and 68736, were employed as carriage shunters at Newcastle and York initially. Both were eventually used at Newcastle, where they always attracted attention.

Fresh from works overhaul, no. 69001 poses for a photograph at Hull Dairycoates. This particular engine was the first to be built by British Railways, being completed at Darlington works in October 1949. No. 69001 was never fitted with a vacuum ejector, it remained in service until September 1963

22.2.55

No. 68681 was photographed at York South depot. This locomotive completed sixty-one years service, being built at Darlington works in 1899. During its long life it remained a steam brake-only engine. Many of the locomotives of this class were used on shunting and short trip workings

23.9.56

In 1922 Armstrong Whitworth & Co. built twenty-five locomotives of the J72 class which were to become nos. 68720–44. Here, no. 68737 stands on the ash-pits at Borough Gardens depot

7.7.56

J52 class 0–6–0ST 3F

This sizeable class of tank locomotives was first introduced by the Great Northern Railway in 1892.

Designer: The earlier engines were of a P. Stirling design, the later ones H.A. Ivatt.

Total built: 137 between 1892 and 1909. Construction was by Doncaster works, Neilson & Co., Robert Stephenson & Co. and Sharp, Stewart & Co. Some were built as class J53 and rebuilt to J52. Numbered 68757–68889.

Principal dimensions

Weight:	Locomotive	51 tons 14 cwt
Boiler pressure:		170 lb/sq in
Driving wheels:		4 ft 8 in
Tractive effort:		21,735 lb
Cylinders:		(2) 18 in x 26 in

Stephenson motion.

These locomotives were a common sight in the London area on shunting work, examples remaining employed until 1959, although a steady stream of engines were making their journey north never to return from the early fifties onwards. The last survivors of the class were in the Leeds area, nos. 68869 and 68875, which were withdrawn in March 1961.

Several of the J52s were used as works shunters at Doncaster works after withdrawal from service stock. The last two, departmental nos. 2 and 9, were withdrawn in February 1961.

One locomotive still survives and is at the National Railway Museum, York. No. 68846 built in 1899 by Sharp, Stewart & Co. was withdrawn in May 1959.

Many J52s were withdrawn from service during the mid-fifties. No. 68885 was one of those to be condemned in September 1956; the engine is seen here at Doncaster awaiting scrapping. Built in 1909, this was one of the final batch

23.9.56

This cast works plate is from J52 no. 68810 and is typical of those fitted to many of the Great Northern goods and shunting locomotives. The Doncaster works no. 740 appears and the locomotive's construction date. Works plates are now very much collectors' items, although in the fifties they could be purchased directly from BR at reasonable prices

This example of the J52 was built at Doncaster in 1894 appearing as class J53, being rebuilt to J52 in 1931 when condensing gear was fitted to this locomotive. It was nearing the end of its days when photographed at its home depot, Colwick. The engine would appear to have received damage to the casing of the second dome, which has a sizeable hole in it. No. 68777 was withdrawn in November 1954

4.4.54

J50 class 0–6–0T 4F

Designer: H.N. Gresley for the Great Northern Railway. Introduced in 1922 (as class J51). These were later rebuilt to J50 class, nos. 68890–919. The engines built from 1922 onwards were all constructed as J50s. There were various detail differences including a development with a larger bunker.
Total built: 102.

Principal dimensions

Weight:	56 tons 6 cwt – 58 tons 3 cwt
Boiler pressure:	175 lb/sq in
Driving wheels:	4 ft 8 in
Tractive effort:	23,635 lb
Cylinders:	(2) 18½ in x 26 in

Stephenson motion.

All locomotives which eventually became, or were built as J50s, were constructed at Doncaster and Gorton works and all came into BR stock, number series 68890–991.

For many years J50s were a familiar sight in the King's Cross area, with Hornsey depot having twenty-seven in its allocation during the mid-fifties. Others were widely distributed throughout the Eastern region. The class remained intact until 1958, the final examples working being withdrawn from stock by 1963. Although a further seven which had been transferred to departmental stock remained in use for another two years, all were withdrawn in May and September of that year. None survive.

This J50, no. 68911, was originally built as a J51 in 1919, being rebuilt to a J50/2 class in August 1930. It was withdrawn in November 1960 when it became departmental no. 10. This locomotive survived for another five years and was eventually condemned in May 1965

Leeds Copley Hill depot, 13.5.56

No. 68980 was one of the batch of J50s built at Gorton works in 1938 designated J50/4, having larger bunkers and fitted with vacuum brakes. In the mid-fifties it was a Doncaster engine, where this picture was taken. No. 68980 was withdrawn in February 1960

23.9.56

N10 class 0–6–2T 3F

Designer: T.W. Worsdell. Introduced in 1902 for the North Eastern Railway.
Total built: 20 at Darlington works between 1902 and 1903. All except one came into British Railways ownership and were numbered 69090–109. In the mid-fifties the highest concentrations were to be found in the Gateshead and Hull areas.

Principal dimensions

Weight:	57 tons 14 cwt
Boiler pressure:	160 lb/sq in
Driving wheels:	4 ft 7¼ in
Tractive effort:	21,905 lb
Cylinders:	(2) 18½ in x 26 in

Stephenson motion.

Withdrawals commenced again in 1955, the only one not to come under BR ownership was withdrawn in 1948. The last three engines, nos. 69097, 69101 and 69109, lasted until April 1962; all three were allocated to Gateshead, ending their days at Darlington works.

No. 69104 prepares to leave Hull Dairycoates depot for its next shunting duty. Note the duty no. 22 plate on the smokebox. This engine was built in 1902 and remained in service until March 1958

22.5.55

Another shot of No. 69104 giving an impression of the 35 ft 7 in overall length of the N10s. Note all the large trailing wheels. Again the duty no. 22 is carried on the back of the coal bunker

22.5.55

N15 class 0–6–2T 4MT

Designer: W.P. Reid. Introduced by the North British Railway in 1910.
Total built: 90 all of which survived to be taken over by British Railways. The N15s were built by the North British Locomotive Co. and R. Stephenson & Co., with the final twenty being built by Cowlairs works between 1923 and 1924. Numbered 69126–69224.

Principal dimensions

Weight:	60 tons 18 cwt (locomotives with smaller bunkers)
Boiler pressure:	175 lb/sq in
Driving wheels:	4 ft 6 in
Tractive effort:	23,205 lb
Cylinders:	(2) 18 in x 26 in
Stephenson motion.	

Six locomotives had large bunkers for use on the difficult 1:42 gradient Cowlairs bank, these being classified N15/2. The N15s were to be found at many Scottish region depots. The first to be withdrawn were in 1957; by 1962 their numbers had been drastically reduced with just twenty-one in service. All were withdrawn during that year, the last, no. 69178, from Motherwell depot in December. Like so many of its classmates it ended its days at Cowlairs works.

Freshly overhauled, no. 69152 stands in the open-tank roundhouse at St Margaret's depot, this engine having received lined-out tanks and coal bunker. It remained in service until December 1958 and, rather surprisingly, was among the first to be withdrawn

21.8.55

N5 class 0–6–2T 2MT

Designer: T. Parker. Introduced in 1891 for the Manchester, Sheffield and Lincolnshire Railway.
Total built: 129 by Gorton works and Beyer, Peacock & Co. between 1891 and 1901. Despite their age 121 survived to be taken over by British Railways and were numbered 69250–370.

Principal dimensions

Weight:	Locomotive	62 tons 7 cwt
Boiler pressure:		160 lb/sq in
Driving wheels:		5 ft 1 in
Tractive effort:		18,780 lb
Cylinders:		(2) 18 in x 26 in

Stephenson motion – slide valves.

Withdrawals of this class, which was the standard shunting locomotive of the Great Central Railway, were heavy from the mid-fifties onwards, increasing numbers of diesel shunters taking over many of its duties. Other locomotives were placed in store and never worked again. Some N5s did survive until 1960, the last one, no. 69307, being withdrawn in December 1960 and cut up at Gorton works the following month.

Several N5s were to be found at Trafford Park depot, including no. 69347 seen here being shunted. This locomotive was built at Gorton in 1900 and remained in service until October 1957. The N5s were the standard shunting locomotives of the Great Central Railway

16.10.55

N8 0–6–2T 2MT

Designer: T.W. Worsdell. Introduced in 1886 for the North Eastern Railway.
Total built: 62.

Principal dimensions

Weight:	58 tons 14 cwt
Boiler pressure:	160 lb/sq in
Driving wheels:	5 ft 1¼ in
Tractive effort:	19,235 lb
Cylinders:	(2) 19 in x 24 in

Stephenson motion.
(The dimensions refer to the last survivor.)

By the end of 1955 only one example of the N8 class remained in traffic, no. 69390. This engine was withdrawn in October 1956.

The last survivor of the N8 class was no. 69390, seen here at Tyne Dock depot. This engine was one of the examples which had been rebuilt with superheater, Stephenson gear and piston valves. No. 69390 was withdrawn in October 1956

7.7.56

N1 class 0–6–2T 2MT

Designer: H.A. Ivatt. Introduced on the Great Northern Railway in 1907.
Total built: 56, all at Doncaster works between 1907 and 1912. Only one failed to be taken over by BR, where they were allocated nos. 69430–85.

Many were fitted with condensing equipment for use in the London area, and in a number of cases this was later removed, the engines concerned going mainly to Yorkshire.

Principal dimensions

Weight:	64 tons 14 cwt
Boiler pressure:	175 lb/sq in (superheated locos 170 lb/sq in)
Driving wheels:	5 ft 8 in
Tractive effort:	17,900 lb (superheated locos)
Cylinders:	(2) 18 in x 16 in

Stephenson motion – slide valves.

Examples of the class were still hard at work in the London area during the early fifties, Hornsey and Hatfield both having a number in their allocation. Many locomotives were withdrawn in 1954 and 1955; in the following year most of the survivors were to be found at sheds in Yorkshire.

The last in service, no. 69462 of Ardsley depot, was withdrawn in April 1959. One N1 was used on stationary boiler duty until December 1962. None survive.

This N1 was originally built with condensing equipment fitted, being completed at Doncaster in March 1910. This particular engine later had the equipment removed. No. 69443 was awaiting its next duty at Bradford depot. It remained in service until March 1959

13.5.56

No. 69435, seen here on the ash-pits at Hornsey depot, was built as a condensing engine, in this case retaining the equipment for its entire life. Built at Doncaster in 1907 this N1 remained in service until March 1955

3.1.54

N2 class 0–6–2T 3MT

Designer: H.N. Gresley. Introduced in 1920.
Total built: 107 over the years 1920–9. The vast majority were built by private companies, four being involved: Beyer, Peacock & Co., Hawthorn, Leslie & Co., North British Locomotive Co. and Yorkshire Engine Co.

Sixteen engines were also built at Doncaster works; all were taken into British Railways stock and numbered 69490–596.

Some of the locomotives were fitted with condensing equipment and shorter chimneys for work in the London area.

Principal dimensions

Weight:	Locomotive:	70–1 tons (depending on fittings)
Boiler pressure:		170 lb/sq in
Driving wheels:		5 ft 8 in
Tractive effort:		19,945 lb
Cylinders:		(2) 19 in x 26 in

Stephenson motion – piston valves.

During the fifties the majority of the class were to be found in the London area where their work included suburban passenger, empty stock and other duties. Examples of the class were to be found as far away as Aberdeen and in the Glasgow area. The King's Cross-based engines continued on suburban workings until 1959, when diesels took over the duties.

Withdrawals began in 1955, but examples were still in service up until 1962 when thirteen engines remained, all of which were withdrawn that year.

One locomotive escaped the cutter's torch: no. 69523, now to be found on the Great Central Railway. This engine was one of the batch built by the North British Locomotive Co. in 1921; withdrawal from service was in September 1962. The engine is now nearing the end of a general overhaul at Loughborough and is expected to be in action again in the near future.

This N2 is an example of the members of the class that were built without condensing gear, in this case by Beyer, Peacock & Co. in 1925. No. 69559 was a Stratford-based engine, remaining in service until July 1957

7.5.55

This locomotive, fitted with condensing equipment, was the first of the class built in 1920 at Doncaster works. When this picture of no. 69490 was taken, on a dull day at a very smoky King's Cross depot, it was ready for its next surburban working. This N2 was a fairly early casualty, being withdrawn in July 1959

3.1.54

N7 class 0–6–2T 3MT

This class consisted of a number of different parts. The first locomotives of the N7 design were built at Stratford in 1915. Other batches were built at Gorton and Doncaster works, as well as by R. Stephenson & Co. and W. Beardmore & Co., the last engine being completed at Doncaster in December 1928.

Designer: A.J. Hill for the Great Eastern Railway; later developed by H.N. Gresley.
Total built: 134. All were handed over to British Railways and allocated number series 69600–733.

Principal dimensions

Weight:	Locomotive	61–4 tons (depending on type)
Boiler pressure:		180 lb/sq in
Driving wheels:		4 ft 10 in
Tractive effort:		20,515 lb
Cylinders:		(2) 18 in x 24 in

Walschaerts motion – piston valves.

Many of these engines were employed on London area suburban services in the early fifties and local workings elsewhere in East Anglia. They, like so many tank engines, were victims of the mass influx of diesel power, both locomotives and multiple units. The first to go was in 1957.

Quite a number still remained in service at the turn of the decade. Seventy-three were withdrawn between 1960 and 1961, leaving just nine. 1962 was to see these also withdrawn, but one is now preserved.

The lucky survivor is no. 69621. After a number of years lying at various locations, including Leeds, this engine is now based at the East Anglian Railway Museum Chapel and Wakes Colne, Essex. On many occasions in the last few years it has been in action in various parts of the country: a very fitting tribute to this popular class.

No. 69601 is an example of the N7/4 class. Built at Stratford in 1915 this was the second locomotive constructed; it was rebuilt to N7/4 specifications with round-topped boiler in 1944. This picture of the engine was taken at its home depot, Stratford. Note the polished ring on the smokebox door and the plain, straight chimney

7.5.55

Visitors to Stratford depot in the mid-fifties were certain to find many examples of the N7 class on shed. No. 69647 is an N7/5 introduced in 1943, a rebuilt N7/1 with round-topped boiler retaining short-travel valves. This locomotive was withdrawn in November 1960

7.5.55

Fresh from general overhaul was N7/3 no. 69727. It was not likely to remain long in this condition at Stratford, the large number of locomotives presenting a very smoky atmosphere. This locomotive survived until November 1960 and was cut up at Stratford eight months later

7.5.55

A7 class 4–6–2T 5F

These heavy tank locomotives were designed principally for short haul duties to and from collieries.
Designer: V. Raven for the North Eastern Railway. Introduced in 1910.
Total built: 20, 1910–11. All were constructed at Darlington works.

Principal dimensions

Weight:	87 tons 10 cwt
Boiler pressure:	(superheated locos) 160 lb/sq in
Driving wheels:	4 ft 7¼ in
Tractive effort:	(superheated) 26,140 lb
Cylinders:	(3) 16½ in x 26 in

Stephenson motion – piston valves.

By 1955 the remaining A7s had been reduced to ten locomotives; the last two, nos. 69772 and 69786, were withdrawn in December 1957. In their final years most of the A7s were to be found at Hull Dairycoates and Springhead depots.

One of the remaining A7s, photographed at Hull Springhead depot. No. 69784 was built in April 1911 and it was in its last year of service, being withdrawn in March 1956. Note the shunter's pole on the buffer beam

22.5.55

A5 class 4–6–2T 4P

Designer: J.G. Robinson. Introduced in 1911 for the Great Central Railway.
Total built: 44. Thirty-one were constructed at Gorton works, 1911–23 and thirteen by Hawthorn Leslie, 1925–6. One locomotive was withdrawn in 1942; the other forty-three were taken over by BR, becoming nos. 69800–42.

These tank locomotives were built in two types, the first appearing from Gorton works. In 1925 a development was introduced, the last thirteen to be constructed having reduced boiler mountings and detail differences, being designated in 1948 A5/2, the original design becoming A5/1.

Principal dimensions

Weight:	A5/1	85 tons 18 cwt
	A5/2	90 tons 11 cwt
Boiler pressure:		180 lb/sq in
Driving wheels:		5 ft 7 in
Tractive effort:		23,700 lb
Cylinders:		(2) 20 in x 26 in

Stephenson motion – piston valves.

In the fifties the A5s were mainly to be found in the Eastern and North Eastern regions (around the Hull area). Their duties consisted mainly of local passenger work for which they were originally built. The A5s were a powerful design, well liked by enginemen. Withdrawals commenced in 1957; within three years all were finished. The last survivors were all Eastern region engines, nos. 69808, 69814 and 68820, being withdrawn in November 1960. They, like the majority of their classmates, ended their days at Darlington works. Unfortunately, none have survived.

No. 69822 stands quietly outside Grantham shed. This engine was an A5/1, built at Gorton in 1923 and withdrawn in November 1958. A5s were frequently used on the Grantham–Nottingham services

7.8.54

This A5, no. 69837, was photographed at Hull Botanic Gardens depot. One of the thirteen A5/2s, it had reduced boiler mountings and detail differences, one of which was a different chimney. The A5/2s were built between 1925 And 1926 by Hawthorn Leslie. This example was withdrawn in December 1958

22.5.55

A8 class 4–6–2T 4P

These locomotives were rebuilds of V. Raven's class D 4–4–4Ts (1913).
Designer: H.N. Gresley. Introduced in 1931.
Total built: 45. The entire class was taken over by British Railways and allocated nos. 69850–94.

Principal dimensions

Weight:	86 tons 18 cwt
Boiler pressure:	175 lb/sq in
Driving wheels:	5 ft 9 in
Tractive effort:	22,940 lb
Cylinders:	(3) 16½ in x 26 in

Stephenson motion – piston valves.

Principally used on passenger work, the powerful A8s were also employed at times on goods or engineers' trains, especially in their later years when many of their earlier duties had been taken over. All were to be found in the North Eastern region allocated to a number of different depots. Indeed from the mid-fifties onwards A8s were to be found in storage or lying temporarily out of use at the back of sheds.

Despite this, the first withdrawals did not take place until 1957. The last survivors lingered on until June 1960, when they were cut up at Darlington works, where the whole class ended its days.

Malton depot's A8, no. 69877, was engaged in working an engineers' train when this picture was taken. Still in good external condition, this engine was rebuilt in December 1925 from an H1 class 4–4–4T which had been built in June 1920. No. 69877 survived until December 1959

22.5.55

Visitors to Darlington during the fifties would usually find one or more A8s present. These locomotives received repairs and overhauls at the works. No. 69861 was pictured in the shed yard; a Malton engine at the time it had possibly arrived for works attention. No. 69861 was withdrawn in June 1960, being among the last survivors of the class

8.7.56

S1 class 0–8–4T 7F

Designer: J.G. Robinson. Introduced in 1907 for the Great Central Railway.
Total built: 6. Four were built between 1907 and 1908 by Beyer, Peacock & Co., and two more in 1932 at Gorton works. All were in service and taken over by British Railways in 1948. The numbers allocated were 69900–5.

Principal dimensions

Weight:	99 tons
Boiler pressure:	180 lb/sq in
Driving wheels:	4 ft 8 in
Tractive effort:	34,525 lb
Cylinders:	(3) 18 in x 26 in

Stephenson valve gear – piston valves.

These massive, heavy tank locomotives were designed for hump shunting work. The class consisted of three parts; class S1/1 were 1907–8 built engines, later rebuilt with superheater; S1/2 no. 69901 was built in 1907 and during its service fitted with a booster which was later removed; S1/3 nos. 69904 and 69905 were the Gorton-built engines completed with boosters when built in 1932, both of these engines having the equipment removed in 1943.

In 1954 no. 69903 was withdrawn; in the same year four others were in store at Doncaster shed, nos. 69900, 69901, 69902 and 69904. During the fifties the class received little work generally. Two exceptions, which were both employed at Frodingham, were nos. 69901 and 69905, these being withdrawn in January 1957, when the class became extinct.

This S1 was one of four stored at Doncaster shed. No. 69902 was an S1/1, built in 1908 by Beyer, Peacock & Co. and never fitted with a booster. When this picture was taken it still carried a Great Central-type chimney. No. 69902 was withdrawn in January 1956

7.11.54

Also in store at Doncaster was no. 69904, an S1/3, one of two built at Gorton works in 1932 and fitted from the outset with boosters which were removed in 1943. This engine was also withdrawn in January 1956. Note the sloping front edge to the tank and side-window cab on this locomotive together with several other detail differences

7.11.54

T1 class 4–8–0T 7F

Designer: T.W. Worsdell. Introduced in 1909 for the North Eastern Railway.
Total built: 15. Ten were built at Gateshead in 1909 and 1910, and five more in 1925 at Darlington works. Thirteen survived to be taken into British Railways stock. Numbered 69910–69917.

Principal dimensions

Weight:	85 tons 8 cwt
Boiler pressure:	175 lb/sq in
Driving wheels:	4 ft 7¼ in
Tractive effort:	34,080 lb
Cylinders:	(3) 18 in x 26 in

Stephenson valve gear – piston valves.

Designed for heavy shunting duties these powerful tank locomotives worked at many marshalling yards in the North East. By the mid-fifties the diesel shunter was taking over many of the duties worked by the T1s, resulting in a number being stored. Withdrawals started in 1955 when nos. 69914 and 69919 were condemned, and continued steadily until 1961 when only no. 69921 remained. In June this engine was also withdrawn from Tyne Dock rendering the class extinct. This final T1 was cut up at Darlington works.

181

In the late fifties T1s were to be found in service at York depot. No. 69910 was pictured in the roundhouse with another classmate alongside. This engine was the first completed in September 1909 at Gateshead works. It remained in service at York until withdrawn in October 1959; the following month it was cut up at Darlington

23.9.56

In 1956 work was becoming scarce for the T1s. Two were in store at Newport, nos. 69911 and 69913. No. 69911 seen here was withdrawn in March 1957. The other engine was transferred to York and withdrawn in December 1957. Note the tarpaulin sheeting covering the chimney, commonplace on stored engines in the past. Also both locomotives' bunkers were full of coal so that they could have been quickly returned to traffic

8.7.56

Q1 class 0–8–0T 5F

Thompson rebuilds of Great Central class Q4 0–8–0s originally introduced in 1902. Rebuilds were Q1/1 class (1,500 gallon tanks) introduced 1942; Q1/2 class (2,000 gallon tanks), 1943.
Designer: E. Thompson.
Total built: 13. All were taken into BR stock and numbered 69925–37.

Principal dimensions

Weight:	Q1/1	69 tons 18 cwt
	Q1/2	73 tons 13 cwt
Boiler pressure:		180 lb/sq in
Driving wheels:		4 ft 8 in
Tractive effort:		25,645 lb
Cylinders:		(2) 19 in x 26 in

Stephenson motion.

Designed for heavy shunting work, as with many other tank locomotives increasing numbers of diesels took over their duties during the fifties. The first to be withdrawn was no. 69925 in 1954, one of two allocated to Eastfield (Glasgow). The last to go were nos. 69935 and 69936 in September 1959 at Frodingham, where the last five in service ended their days. Some spent lengthy periods in store. None survive.

No. 69927 was one of two Q1/1 classes allocated to Eastfield depot. This locomotive was rebuilt from a Q4 0–8–0 in December 1942. Only four of the thirteen Q1s were of the part one type with 1,500 gallon tanks, carrying nos. 69925–8

26.8.58

Five of these massive 0–8–0Ts ended their days at Frodingham; all were Q1/2 class with 2,000 gallon tanks. In the final years many were to spend time in store. No. 69934 was one of these; it was rebuilt in September 1944, withdrawn in August 1959 and cut up at Darlington the following month

Frodingham, 25.8.57